LAURA

America's First Lady, First Mother

Antonia Felix

Adams Media Corporation
Avon, Massachusetts

Published by
Adams Media Corporation
57 Littlefield Street, Avon, MA 02322 U.S.A.
www.adamsmedia.com

ISBN: 1-58062-659-9

Printed in the United States of America.

J I H G F E D C B A

Felix, Antonia.
    Laura : America's first lady, first mother / by Antonia Felix.
      p.   cm.
    Includes bibliographical references.
    ISBN 1-58062-659-9
    1. Bush, Laura Welch, 1946- 2. Presidents' spouses--United States--Biog-
raphy. 3. Mothers--United States--Biography. 4. Bush, Laura Welch, 1946--
Family. I. Title.
    E904.B87 F45 2002
    973.934'092—dc21   2001055210
    [B]

Photos reprinted with permission on black and white insert with credit
of Jenna Welch Collection, George Bush Library, Janice Price Collection,
and Randolph Rubin Collection are courtesy of The Petroleum Museum,
Midland, Texas. Other photos are reprinted with permission noted.

*This book is available at quantity discounts for bulk purchases.
For information, call 1-800-872-5627.*

CONTENTS

❖

To Jenna Louise Hawkins Welch,
mother of Laura Welch Bush

❖

Author's Note
and Acknowledgments

I SUBMITTED THIS MANUSCRIPT to the publisher in late August 2001, but with the tragic events of September 11th, I asked my editor, Claire Gerus, to allow me to add a new section about the First Lady's efforts to bring calm and healing to our wounded nation. The result is additional material that chronicles Laura Bush's experiences on that hellish day and the many appearances and speeches she made in the days and weeks that followed. Before the tragedy, few people knew much about Laura Bush, but her subsequent media appearances sent a warm, personal, and utterly sincere message to parents, teachers, and children throughout the country, helping them cope with pain that words cannot describe.

I was in Manhattan on September 11, but my home is in Midtown, far from the financial district where the towers once stood. Thankfully, my friends who work in the area all made it out alive. I was never more proud to be a New Yorker than on that day and during the weeks that followed, as everyone slowly emerged from their daze, refused to let their spirits be broken—although their hearts were—and got on with the work that brought us all here. And I, like all New Yorkers, was never more proud of our mayor, Rudolph Giuliani, who wore his heart on his sleeve and rallied every ounce of his no-frills intensity and energy to bolster our spirits and calm our fragile nerves.

As a result of the First Lady's new prominence as America's "First Mother" in the wake of these tragic events, I am even more grateful to have had the opportunity to present her story.

I extend warm thanks and gratitude to Laura's mother, Jenna Welch, for her generous time and cooperation in granting me interviews. I am also deeply indebted to Todd Houck of Midland, Texas, Laura Bush's hometown. A historian at the Petroleum Museum in Midland, Todd was an invaluable source of information and insights about the town, the region, and the family, as well as the oil industry that put West Texas on the map. My thanks also go to Bruce Partain, formerly of the Midland Chamber of Commerce, and to all the friendly people of Midland who made my time there so memorable.

I also thank Claire Gerus, my editor at Adams Media, for making this book possible and for all of her valuable input; my agent Tony Seidl, who always keeps his eyes open for an interesting project; and my husband, Stanford, who, in spite of his busy schedule as a new professor at Texas A&M, took the time to read and offer much-appreciated comments on the first drafts of this book.

First Lady:
September 11, 2001

"I think every American has been comforted and reassured by Mrs. Bush."
—SENATOR HILLARY RODHAM CLINTON

L AURA BUSH GOT UP THAT MORNING with eager—if not a little nervous—anticipation. Today she would appear before a Senate committee and take the issue to which she was devoted to a whole new level. Echoing her previous appearances with Texas legislators, she would now testify to national lawmakers about the country's desperate need for improved early childhood education. Now, by stepping officially into a national forum, the First Lady could improve the lives of even more American children.

Tuesday, September 11, 2001, had all the earmarks of a very good day. The sun rose brightly, and at roughly 8:45 A.M. that morning, Laura Bush stepped into a car in an official motorcade headed to the office of Senator Edward Kennedy, chairman of the Senate Committee on Health, Education, Labor and Pensions.

❖ ❖ ❖

WITHIN MINUTES of stepping into the car, Laura heard the heart-stopping news: a commercial jet had crashed into the North Tower at New York's World Trade Center. Moments later, while en route to Senator Kennedy's office, word came of the second attack—this time on the South Tower.

The chilling news was difficult to absorb: Within eighteen minutes, the World Trade Center was not only under attack, but aflame, with thousands of casualties and panic in the streets.

Hastening into the Senator's office, Laura was greeted by her grim-faced, shaken host. Both sat down to hear the updates of a tragedy that was assuming epic proportions. In both their minds were the questions, "What next?" Is this an isolated attack, or are more on the way?" And overriding all, the sense of horror at innocent lives lost on a day when most Americans were least expecting to become widows, orphans, and widowers.

Numbly, both Laura and Senator Kennedy struggled to absorb the news as updates poured in. Finally, realizing that America needed to hear from its senior officials, they shakily rose and addressed the journalists who had assembled to cover the committee meeting.

"Our hearts and our prayers go out to the victims of this act of terrorism," Laura said solemnly. Then, turning instinctively to a subject that would become familiar in days to come, she urged, "Parents need to reassure their children everywhere in our country that they're safe."

Senator Kennedy stressed that the terrorists had not disrupted the work of the committee but merely delayed it. "We are not going to see the business of America deferred because of terrorism, whether it's in education or another area of public policy," he said defiantly.

Laura finally heard from her husband when he called her from Sarasota, Florida before making his first television appearance to the nation. After a private conversation, during which they shared their shock and tried to reassure each other, George W. Bush made his address to the nation. At 9:30 A.M., only forty-five minutes after the strike in New York City, he told Americans, "We have had a national tragedy. Two airplanes have crashed into the World Trade Center in an apparent terrorist attack on our country."

Thirteen minutes after the president made his announcement, Washington became the third target when another hijacked airliner crashed into the Pentagon and exploded. With news of the local attack, the First Lady and Senator Kennedy were hurriedly escorted to a holding room in the basement by a team of Secret Service agents.

From there, Laura and her aides were rushed out of the building and into a waiting limousine as hundreds of people, urged to evacuate, hurried down the steps. Laura and her group were driven to a secret location where they huddled around a television set to watch the nightmare unfold.

"The first thing I did was to call my girls to let them know they were safe," said Laura. "Then I called my mother. She thinks I called to reassure her that I was okay, but the fact is, I called to hear her voice. My mother, in her generation, lived through something very similar, the attack on Pearl Harbor. I knew she could be reassuring."[1]

Later, Laura's mother would say, "When I heard her say on television that she called to hear my reassuring voice, I was surprised," she said. "I thought it was the other way around."

Laura and her staff sat together, transfixed, in front of the television as one scene after another delivered blow after blow.

8:48. American Airlines Flight 11 crashes into the North Tower of the World Trade Center

9:03. A second hijacked jet, this time United Airlines Flight 175, drives into the South Tower

9:43. The Pentagon is hit by American Airlines Flight 77, a third hijacked airliner.

10:05. The South Tower of the World Trade Center collapses.

10:10. Another hijacked airliner, this time a United Airlines flight, crashes southeast of Pittsburgh.

10:28. The World Trade Center's North Tower collapses.

The grim statistics followed: On an average workday, from 20,000 to 40,000 people worked in the towers. How many of them had survived? Gazing at the inferno, and the collapsing buildings, it was hard to imagine that any could walk out of there alive.

Meanwhile, after making his brief remarks to the press, the president was flown from Florida to Barksdale Air Force Base in Louisiana, then to another base in Nebraska. Americans began worrying: Why wasn't he heading back to the White House?

Finally, overriding the advice of his security team, he insisted on returning to Washington. At 4:30 P.M., a shaken but determined George W. Bush boarded Air Force One and flew to Washington with an escort of three fighter jets. That day, and for days to follow, Air Force fighter jets would be seen streaking through New York and Washington air space while buildings burned in New York's financial district and in the nation's capital.

The unimaginable had hit the nation with a vengeance. Nothing would ever be the same.

❖   ❖   ❖

SEPTEMBER 11TH was to have been a historic day for First Lady Laura Bush. She was about to become the fourth First Lady to testify before a senate committee. Before her, Eleanor

Roosevelt had appealed to Congress to deplore the conditions of Washington's public schools and hospitals. Then, Rosalynn Carter had testified about the need for a better mental health policy, which led to the passage of the 1980 Mental Health Systems Act. And almost exactly eight years ago, Hillary Rodham Clinton had appeared before five house and senate committees to present the details of her health care bill.

But rather than mark the groundbreaking appearance of Laura Bush's senate testimony, September 11th would instead become the darkest day in the nation's history.

First Families have always drawn on each other's strength to endure tragedy in the past. Today, however, was a day that would challenge even the most stalwart family to keep its faith, and its sanity, in the face of such overwhelming terror.

And for Laura Bush, the challenge would be a test of her faith—and of her ability to remain the calm, serene "rock" in her husband's life.

CHAPTER 1

The Girl
from West Texas

"West Texas commands the respect of its inhabitants. If one thing could be said of those whose lives and livelihoods revolve around the place, it is that they don't simply live on or off the land; they live with it—and thrive."

—LAURA BUSH, FROM THE FOREWORD TO *WHATEVER THE WIND DELIVERS*

O N JANUARY 20, 2001, millions of Americans tuned in to television coverage of the Fifty-second Presidential Inaugural Ball. The new president, George W. Bush, was a familiar face as the recent two-term governor of Texas and son of a former president. But the woman dancing with him—striking with her short chestnut hair and sparkling blue eyes, and dressed in a red Chantilly lace evening gown—was a new face to most Americans.

Many wondered who this new First Lady was—and what impact she would have after the precedent set by Hillary Clinton, who had just won one of the most historic Senate races in history and was moving her office from the White House to Capitol Hill.

Now, as viewers watched the First Couple sweep across the dance floor, the questions arose: Does the new First Lady have her own political agenda? Has she, like Hillary Rodham Clinton, come to Washington as her husband's political partner? What issues does she hope to work with in her new role? Where does Laura Bush come from—is hers a prominent New England family, like that of her husband and mother-in-law? Does she have a career?

And, finally, would she be able to bring a softer, gentler, more nurturing image to the position of First Lady?

Everyone has a distinctive persona that defines his or her public image, and the persona of a political wife is often carefully constructed. But beneath that exterior lies a personal history shaped by one's parents, hometown, ambitions, loves, and decisions.

Laura Welch Bush was strongly shaped by her West Texas beginnings. To understand her, you have to know something about her father, Harold, and her mother, Jenna. You have to explore a little of the history of Midland, Texas, her hometown. And you have to recognize how all these influences shaped the girl who would one day have the second most powerful position in America: First Lady to the Forty-third President of the United States.

❖   ❖   ❖

LAURA BUSH began life as a "fortunate daughter." She was fortunate because she grew up in the early 1950s in a comfortable Texas town where crime was nearly nonexistent and wholesome events such as the World Championship Rodeo Day were eagerly anticipated by young and old alike.

She was also fortunate to have a solid, affectionate mother and a father who loved to laugh. As a result, the Welch house was a popular haven for Laura and her friends. There was no need to escape to a mall, or to roam the streets looking for something to do. Everything Laura and her friends might have wanted was right here.

Harold Welch—ambitious and extroverted—was a lot like the man his daughter would marry. George W. Bush once described his father-in-law as "a gentle, decent man. He didn't have a mean bone in his body."

As Harold pursued a successful career in home building,

Jenna pitched in to help her husband, taking on the roles of accountant and bookkeeper. She insisted on working from home so she could properly care for young Laura, their first and only child, who was born on November 4, 1946.

From the beginning, Laura was a delightful addition to the family. "She was an easy baby," recalled Jenna. "She never cried and she was hardly even sick."[1] The calm, contented personality that strikes everyone who meets Laura Bush was evident from babyhood, according to her mother, who added that her daughter was "just born a happy little kiddo."[2]

Although Jenna and Harold Welch had wanted to raise a large family, unfortunately it was not meant to be. From early on, young Laura sensed that her parents wanted other children. She said, "I was very aware that that was one of the disappointments—that they didn't have a lot of children."[3]

❖ ❖ ❖

JENNA WELCH had also been an only child, but her mother, Jessie, had come from a family of seven sisters. Jessie's mother, Eva, had been widowed at an early age, but was fortunate to have started a successful dairy farm that kept her and her girls busy with daily chores. The girls fed and milked the cows, cleaned out the barn, bottled milk, loaded products onto the delivery wagon, and drove the horse-drawn wagon to customers within a wide radius of the farm.

In fact, one day, while delivering milk with one of her daughters, Eva spotted a mailman coming toward them from the opposite direction. She casually mentioned him to her daughter,

Jessie Laura, and as they passed each other, the young pair turned towards each other. Jessie would eventually marry her postman, Harold Hawkins, and they would have a daughter, Jenna, who would also one day marry a Harold.

Jenna considered herself lucky to have found her Harold, a man whose laughter lit up a room. Laura observed her mother's devotion to her husband and her family. But Jenna was a multi-faceted woman, and Laura once observed that her mother was a woman "of that generation who really wanted to please her husband, and cooked three meals a day. . . . But she also was very interested in a lot of things outside of her marriage. When we got our Girl Scout bird badges, she was the Girl Scout leader and she developed a great interest in bird-watching."[4]

A love for nature came easily to Jenna. As she grew up, she had developed a passion for the wildflowers of West Texas. "My mother [Laura's grandmother] grew up on a farm in Arkansas," she recalls, "and we often talked about flowers and birds. She was sort of a self-taught naturalist, and I'm the same way."

Her love for birds continued after moving to Midland, where she joined the Midland Naturalist Group. "We put out a wonderful monthly publication, the *Phalarope*, which reports on nature in the area. They named the newsletter after the phalarope, a water bird that swims around in a circle to stir up the water and make the fish come up. The female also runs off on little errands of her own and leaves the male to care for the young. The women in the group liken themselves to the phalarope—they stir things up in the nature-loving community and leave their husbands at home at times to go birding."

Laura's mother "stirred things up" as a naturalist, working

to improve the environment, and years later, her daughter would display some of her mother's "phalarope" qualities when, as First Lady, she would "stir up" the education system's kettle to improve schooling for America's children.

As she moved through her childhood, Laura found security and strength in the delights of daily life in Midland, the small Texas town that would soon become a thriving center for oil interests. In time, this phenomenon would not only affect her family, but it would create the setting for a meeting with the man who would one day become her husband.

❖   ❖   ❖

OIL WAS TO be the bridge that would connect Laura's past with her future. The presence of oil was, in fact, one reason why her father, Harold Welch, had chosen to settle in Texas in 1946 after completing a four-year stint with the Army. Harold had just returned to the United States from Germany, where he had spent his last days with the Army's 555th Anti-Aircraft Battalion trying to survive a difficult winter. He and his mates had fought in the bitter cold by day, and slept in freezing, bombed-out houses at night. Memories of that bone-chilling cold and blinding snow would haunt Laura's father for the rest of his life.

At last, with the surrender of Germany on January 2, 1946, Harold Welch gratefully went home to his wife, Jenna Louise Hawkins Welch, whom he had married during one of his leaves in 1944.

Now back in the United States, Harold discovered that the war years had been good to nearby Midland, Texas. Since early 1942, it had been the site of the Army Air Force Bombardier

Training School, the largest military training facility in the world.

Between April 1942 and January 1945, more than 6,000 cadets had flown practice bombing runs over the West Texas desert. About half of those cadets had young wives and children, and neither the base nor the town of Midland had enough homes for them. Adding to the housing crunch was a new influx of oil companies that chose to set up shop in Midland because of its accessibility and central location in the oil basin.

Midland's housing shortage was actually a boon for Harold Welch, whose father had been a builder in Lubbock, Texas. From his father, Harold had inherited the desire to create something from the ground up. He decided to use his spare time to learn more about the building business, while carrying a full time job as a district manager of five branches of the Universal CIT Credit Corp, an institution, explains his widow, Jenna, that financed automobile dealers.

Eventually he resigned from his job as a credit officer and went into building and developing full-time. He formed a business with another Midland builder, Lloyd Waynick, and their company enjoyed a significant portion of Midland's residential expansion over the next twenty years, including the development of five major subdivisions encircling the growing city.

"Lloyd and Harold's company, Waynick and Welch, built about 200 homes in Midland," Jenna Welch proudly remembers. "The development on Humble Street, including the house where we lived when Laura was in high school, was a cotton field when they bought it."

The house Harold built for his family on Humble Street was one of his most popular designs, a one-story three-bedroom with wood-beam cathedral ceilings, a den with a fireplace, and a large, airy kitchen. "In the 1970s those houses cost about $25,000," said Jenna. "Later he built bigger, four-bedroom homes."

Harold's background in designing homes came from two sources: watching his father and using his imagination. "Harold just liked building," recalls Jenna. "He would take a piece of paper and draw up a floor plan and then take it to a draftsman who would make a blueprint. His big four-bedroom plan was really wonderful, and he built a lot of those homes."[5]

Midland's rise to prominence in the oil world began in 1926, when Gulf Oil Company was the first of several big oil companies to move its operations there. In three years, West Texas's first "skyscraper," the twelve-story Petroleum Building, soared above the rest of Midland. The Permian Basin's first oil boom ended with the Depression of the 1930s, when big oil discoveries in East Texas caused oil companies to pull out of Midland and head to the newest fields. But drilling resumed in the mid-1930s and throughout the Second World War, bringing the oil companies back into Midland and launching a huge period of growth for the town.

Then, between 1945 and 1950, a series of big oil strikes just south of Midland known as the Spraberry discovery brought more than 11,000 people into Midland. The oil boom of the 1940s had also attracted an ambitious young war hero from Connecticut.

George Herbert Walker Bush was also attracted to the promise of oil in the Southwest, and left Connecticut to find just the right location. He settled on Midland in 1950, where he became a salesman for an oil-drilling equipment company.

Bush brought with him his wife, Barbara, their two-year-old son, George W., and their infant daughter, Robin.

The Bush family's first home was in a neighborhood called Easter Egg Row. "Every brand-new, identical house was painted a different wild color and cost just under $8,000," recalled Barbara Bush in her autobiography. "We loved that marvelous little home."[6]

The Bushes had settled into the same part of town as the Welches, who, with their three-year-old daughter, Laura, lived about fifteen blocks south of Easter Egg Row on Estes Avenue. The two families were not yet destined to meet, however. They attended different churches—the Bushes went to First Presbyterian and the Welches to First Methodist—and did not yet know each other.

In 1950, the Welches entered Laura in a private kindergarten called Alyne Gray's Jack and Jill. At the end of her first week, Laura impressed her mother (as well as herself) with her excellent memory. "She prided herself in the first week of school by learning the names of all the children in her class," recalled Jenna Welch.

Remembering names was a skill Laura would use throughout her career as a teacher and librarian. "When she was school librarian," continued her mother, "she had seven hundred kids in the school, and she tried to learn the names of as many as she could. As to the kindergarten children that came in every day that she read to, she learned their names right off."[7]

When she was five years old, Laura took a ballet class at a popular Midland studio run by Georgia Harston. She also began swimming lessons at that age, joining a beginner's class at

Hogan Park in the northeast section of town. To top off an already active schedule, young Laura joined the cherub choir.

"They only sang in church once or twice a year, but they went every week for choir practice," recalls Laura's mother. "The children learned discipline as well as how to read music. Laura sang in the church choir until the eighth grade, and this training helped her when she got to college and studied the music courses that all education majors are required to take."[8]

After first grade, Laura spent the rest of her school years in the Midland public school system. Like many American small towns in the 1950s, Midland was a place safe enough for young children to walk the streets by themselves. It also offered seasonal treats to its residents. In the summer, everyone went downtown to watch the parades on the Fourth of July, and during World Championship Rodeo days, cowboys and rodeo clowns from the annual spectacle made their way through the town to the cheers of enthusiastic onlookers.

Midland in the 1950s was the business center for oil companies in West Texas. Before the discovery of oil in the 1920s, the town had earned its place on the map as the midpoint along the Texas and Pacific Railroad that connected the cattle country in the West to the commercial centers in the East. Known as "Midway" in those days, the town lay equidistant between Fort Worth and El Paso, the railroad's beginning and end points.

Building a railroad across Texas—the first step in opening the land to prosperity through ranching and other industries—was only possible after the Native Americans had been driven from the Plains. In 1859, after the failure of the reservations and on the heels of encroaching white settlement, all Comanches were ordered out of Texas to Native American territory in the north, an area that is now Oklahoma. Laura Welch Bush's mother, Jenna, was born about forty years later—the battle-scarred frontier history of West Texas a lingering memory to those of her generation.

The explosion of westward expansion after the discovery of gold in California and the elimination of the Native Americans fueled the need for a railroad through Texas, which, because of its mild winter climate, was one of the most popular routes for pioneer wagon trains. Midway was an important stop along the route of the Texas and Pacific Railroad.

The first permanent resident of Midway was a sheep farmer named Herman Garrett, who arrived with his herd in 1882. Two years later Midway was renamed "Midland" in order to obtain a post office, as the name Midway had already been used. Among other early sheep ranchers was John Scharbauer who would team up with his brothers to organize the Scharbauer Cattle Company at the turn of the century. Clarence Scharbauer built the Hotel Scharbauer in Midland in 1927, an enormous and luxurious hotel that served as the center of cattle and oil deal-making. More deals of this kind were made with handshakes in the Scharbauer lobby than anywhere else in the country. Sometimes a prized cow or two stood on display in the lobby, munching fresh hay and making quite an attraction. The hotel was eventually named a Texas landmark, but in 1973, nine years after Laura Welch graduated from high school, the Scharbauer was razed to make way for a fourteen-floor Hilton hotel.

The railroad made Midland one of the biggest cattle shipping towns in the state. Nearly 120 years later, when Laura Welch Bush stood with her husband on a platform in downtown Midland for a presidential victory party in January 2000, the train whistle that she had listened to several times a day while growing up cut through the din of the festivities. Like the wind and the dust, trains remain a constant in Midland, Texas.

Todd Houck, a historian and Director of Archives at Midland's Petroleum Museum, remembers Midland as "the typical, Norman Rockwell kind of world. Everyone felt very safe. No one would dare bring a lighter into school, much less a gun."

Laura was a typical Texas schoolgirl. Once a week, she would put on her Brownie Scouts uniform and wear it to James Bowie Elementary school. After the last bell, she would walk with a few of her friends to Mrs. Smith's house for their troop meeting.

There, her Brownie Scout leaders, Mrs. Barrett and Mrs. Smith, taught the girls simple household skills interlaced with basic lessons in citizenship, as outlined in the *Brownie Scouts Handbook*. Like hundreds of thousands of other Brownies across the country, Laura and her troop began each meeting by reciting the Brownie Promise: *I promise to do my best, to love God and my country, to help other people every day, especially those at home.*

Recalls one of her fellow Scouts: "My mother and Gwyne Smith's mom spent one afternoon each week trying to mold a lively group of seven-year-olds into domestic young ladies," said Martha Barrett Schleicher. "Laura was one of my mom's favorites because she listened quietly and followed directions well."[9]

Another childhood friend, Sally Brady Rock, reminisced about her troop meetings with Laura. "I remember Brownie Scout meetings over at Gwyne Smith's house," she said, "and our little arts and crafts projects that we would do. She [Laura] was always so good. She always made things well. . . ."[10]

Laura not only was well behaved, but she learned from her mentors. From the tender age of seven, she knew what she wanted to be when she grew up. Inspired by her second grade teacher, Mrs. Charlene Gnagy, she told her parents that she, too, wanted to be a teacher. Decades later she would invite her beloved second-grade instructor to her husband's inauguration, and place her in the front row at the White House ceremony.

Young Laura loved "rehearsing" to become a teacher. In fact, her mother recalled one typical episode during Laura's grade school days when she and a friend were playing school at her house. Each girl had set up a class in one of the bedrooms, but instead of attending to their students, they were standing in the hallway, talking.

Laura's mother asked them why they were in the hall. "I thought you were teaching your classes," she inquired of Laura and her friend.

With her usual spunk, Laura replied that she was, indeed playing teacher. "This is what our teachers do!"[11]

At the age of eight, Laura graduated to Girl Scouts and attended her first summer camp. It was almost 200 miles away from home in the Davis Mountains southwest of Midland—a beautiful valley nestled between two plateaus, with an unparalleled view of Mitre Peak. Coyotes, turkey buzzards, deer, wild turkeys, jackrabbits, and other animals live in the wilderness surrounding the camp.

But Laura wasn't ready to leave home for so long. "She went for just a week," said Laura's mother. "Then she asked to come home. I think she was homesick. She wouldn't go back for a year or two."

Laura had forged a strong bond with her parents and friends, and found being apart from them very difficult. But when she was older, she returned to the camp, and this time, she truly enjoyed herself. She also spent summers camping at Bandera, 370 miles southeast of Midland, a ranching center in the Texas Hill Country known as the "Cowboy Capital of the World."

"We had a great time in scouts," said Laura's mother, who was one of her Scout leaders. "We organized things to do around the community and took the girls on field trips.

"The summer between her junior and senior year in college," said her mother, "Laura was a camp counselor at Camp Mystic in the Texas Hill Country Northwest of San Antonio. She had a good time—and earned a little money, too."[12]

Camping with the Girl Scouts had given Laura an introduction to nature and outdoor adventure that became an essential part of her life. Later, as First Lady of Texas, one of her favorite getaways was taking white-water rafting trips with friends.

The summer temperatures in Midland can reach into the 100s, and Laura spent many days at the swimming pool with her friends. Afterwards, Laura would bring a friend or two home to visit or to spend the night. Laura's house was a center of liveliness and good humor. Her friends felt right at home, thanks to her father's quick wit and her mother's warm welcome.

"You always loved to hang out at their house," said one of Laura's best friends, Jan Donnelly O'Neill. "You just always laughed and had a good time . . . sitting down and having Cokes with Laura and her mom and dad."[13]

Laura fondly recalls her father's sense of humor. "My daddy loved to laugh," she said. "He loved animals. He was just one of those men who never met a dog he didn't like or that didn't like him. He was funny and didn't take himself too seriously."[14]

According to those who have known her most of her life, Laura inherited her father's sense of humor. Her mother acknowledges that Laura has a unique sense of humor, but isn't sure exactly where it came from.

"Are we born with a sense of humor or do we develop it?" she mused in an interview. "I'm not sure, but Laura has always had a subtle sense of humor. Her father was much the same way."

On weekends the girls took turns staying over at each other's houses, and sometimes a group would get together for a slumber party. Many Friday nights, Laura slept over at the home of her friend Gwyne Smith or Gwyne stayed over at the Welches'.

Laura's friends knew that she had two great loves: reading and pets. One of her childhood friends, Judy Jones Ryan, gave Laura her first kitten when they were little girls. "I remember he had a real pug nose, kind of flat, and she would always push on his nose. It was a tabby, and she loved it. . . ."

Laura's dog, a mixed-breed named Marty, became Laura's constant companion. Another friend recalled finding Laura in the back yard one summer day, ridding Marty of his wood ticks without being the least bit grossed out.

"She was picking off ticks and putting them in a solution very methodically," said Peggy Porter Weiss. "I was thinking, 'Oh, my gosh, I would never do this, and if someone forced me to do this, I would complain the whole time.'"

Laura looked up and told her squeamish friend, "It's not so bad!"[15]

After spending her first school years at North Elementary and Bowie Elementary, Laura entered San Jacinto Junior High. Friends recalled that Laura went out of her way to make sure that the kids who transferred from one of the smaller parochial elementary schools were accepted by the students who had spent all their elementary years together.

"I was rather intimidated by all of the others in school," said Cindy Schumann Klatt, who had spent her first eight years of school at neighboring St. Ann's. "My first memory of Laura is how friendly and concerned she was that those of us from St. Ann's were included in activities around school."

Another new friend in junior high, Karen Thompson Trout, described Laura as "a very, very sweet girl. She always was a friend to everybody."[16]

❖   ❖   ❖

WHEN LAURA started high school in 1961, she was in the first 10th grade class to attend the area's new Robert E. Lee High School. Always the literary type, she worked on the yearbook and signed up for honors classes.

But Laura Welch enjoyed an active social life, too. She always seemed to have a date for the post-game victory dances, which the school held whether or not their home team, the Rebels, had won.

And the place to go post-game, or any time the teens felt the urge to hang out with their crowd, was Agnes's drive-in. Recalled Laura's longtime friend Jan Donnelly O'Neill, who has known her for forty years: "We could drive at fourteen at that point, so you know, you would take the family car and go and get a Coke and kind of hang out at the '50s-style drive-ins."[17]

"There were at least five girls in the car every time we went out," added Peggy Weiss, another of Laura's lifelong friends. "We liked Kent cigarettes and would be down on the floor in the back of the car, smoking. We all stopped smoking eventually."[18]

Laura has often expressed her appreciation for the innocent, cozy lifestyle she enjoyed in Midland. "I was lucky to have a very normal childhood in a small town where people felt free to do whatever [they] wanted to do. We were sheltered in this freedom in a way that maybe we didn't understand."[19]

Between her sophomore and junior years, Laura and a group of friends from Lee High took a trip to Monterrey, Mexico. They spent the summer taking a Spanish language and cultural studies course. Monterrey, about 145 miles south of the Texas border, is the third largest city in Mexico and, with many English-speaking residents and American stores is more like a Southwest American city than any other city in Mexico.

The rugged beauty of the Sierra Madre mountains formed the backdrop for Laura and her friends' casual strolls and tours of Monterrey's seventeenth and eighteenth century architecture. They took classes during the day and, back in their dorm rooms, devised their own Spanish vocabulary lessons: listening to pop songs on the radio and trying to make out the words.

Even though they lived in the same town, Laura and George W. Bush did not meet while they were growing up. President Bush told one journalist that he was certain they had met in the seventh grade—the one year they both attended the same school, San Jacinto Junior High—but Laura, with her impeccable memory, does not recall ever having met him at that time.

During her high school years, however, Laura did take part in a YMCA program that indirectly connected her to the Bush family. She participated in Tri-Hi-Y, a leadership and character-building organization for high school women. Coincidentally, in 1953, George H. Bush was one of the founders of the Midland YMCA. Now, his contribution to the youth of Midland was already enhancing the life of his future daughter-in-law.

Tri-Hi-Y is the girls' offshoot of Hi-Y, a YMCA organization for high school–age boys created in 1889. The first Tri-Hi-Y was launched by girls in Holyoke, Massachusetts in 1924.

"The mission of this youth program is to invite young women to take a look at their communities and find out what they can do to make them a better place," said David King, Executive Director of the Hi-Y Leadership Center in St. George, West Virginia. "They learn how to assess their skills to use what they have to make a difference where they are. The focus is on leadership, personal character, responsibility, and providing service to the community. From the beginning, the philosophy of Hi-Y and Tri-Hi-Y held that a leader is not necessarily someone who stands out in front and gives great speeches. A civic leader is also the person who is on the bottom helping lift up instead of on the top giving orders."[20]

That philosophy clearly resonates with Laura Welch Bush's style of public service. (Later, she would tell her fiancé, George, that she preferred working quietly behind the scenes.) Never did she run for political office in school or in college. She did, however, focus on learning how to "lift" her children up, one at a time, as their teacher.

Other prominent national figures who took part in Hi-Y

have been Ronald Reagan, who was vice president of his Hi-Y
at Dixon High School in Dixon, Illinois, and John Glenn, who
was a member of Hi-Y as a student at New Concord High
School in Ohio.

Midland's Lee High was ushering in new academic challenges for its students in the 1960s, and in Laura's senior year
she took a new honors class, History of Western Thought. It
was an advanced course that gave Laura a head start when she
started college at Southern Methodist University. Her mother
recalled that the honors class "had an extensive reading list, but
it really helped her when she got to college the next year."[21]

Academics, Tri-Hi-Y, reading, and her involvement in the
First Methodist Church were Laura's major occupations in high
school, but she was hardly a bookworm. A well-rounded student, she enjoyed swimming and hiking, and looked forward to
those opportunities when she could simply be outdoors.

One year, she took part in an event that gave her and other
young ladies of Lee High School an excuse to rough it up on the
football field—they participated in a powder puff football game
against the rival Midland High School. Also known as "women's
flag football" among today's serious players, the game involved
role reversals for the students, with the girls donning soccer-like
uniforms and the boys dressing in cheerleader outfits.

Laura's high school years, filled with friendship and a
close, loving relationship with her parents, did bring one serious
setback—a tragic accident in her senior year. Shortly after 8 P.M.
on November 6, 1963—two days after her seventeenth
birthday—Laura came to an intersection while driving her
Chevrolet sedan on the outskirts of town. Her friend, Judy
Dykes, was in the passenger seat. Laura went through the stop

sign and hit another car, a Corvair sedan that she would later learn was driven by her close friend, Michael Douglas.

Seventeen-year-old Michael was thrown from his car and killed, and a shaken Laura and Judy were taken to the hospital, where they were treated for minor injuries. The police report stated that neither driver was drinking, and no charges were filed in the case.

"Nobody here held it against her," said a Midland friend, Robert McCleskey.[22] But a grief-stricken Laura stayed home from school for a week after the accident, and the entire town reeled as a result of this terrible accident.

"It was as if two of Midland's favorites had been involved in an unthinkable act of fate," said Midland resident Jack Hickman in a television biography about Laura. "He [her father] would have taken that hurt for her if he could."[23]

The story was publicized by the national press in January 2000, when George W. was campaigning as a presidential nominee for the Republican party. Although clearly painful for Laura to recall, she confronted the accident—and her part in it—in interview after interview.

> I grieved a lot. It was a horrible, horrible tragedy. It's a terrible feeling to be responsible for an accident. And it was horrible for all of us to lose him, especially since he was so young. But at some point I had to accept that death is a part of life, and as tragic as losing Mike was, there was nothing anyone could do to change that. . . . It was a comeuppance. At that age, you think you're immortal, invincible. You never expect to lose anybody you love when you're so young. For all of us, it was a

shock. It was a sign of the preciousness of life and how fleeting it can be.[24]

Harold and Jenna Welch could not take away Laura's pain, but the close relationship they had with their daughter helped her heal over time. They were a solid, down-to-earth family, and the accident summoned up in Laura the strength to go on—a strength that would be called upon again, in future years, during other personal strains and setbacks.

❖ ❖ ❖

HAROLD WELCH died at the age of eighty-two on April 29, 1995, from Alzheimer's disease, just months after seeing his daughter become First Lady of Texas. His funeral was held two days later at the First United Methodist Church and he was buried at Resthaven Memorial Park, a cemetery in the northeast corner of Midland.

Since Harold's death, Jenna has lived in their home on Humble Avenue and continues to visit friends and go about her usual routine. She drives down to the corner of Main and Ohio every Sunday to attend services at First United Methodist where she taught Sunday school for many years; travels to Washington or the ranch in Crawford, Texas, to visit the Bushes from time to time; and drives to visit friends in the Midland-Odessa area and in her hometown of El Paso.

Like her daughter, Jenna Welch is low-key and unassuming. Her friend, Todd Houck, recalled leaving a meeting with her one evening.

"I helped her over to her car," he said, "and she opened the passenger door and, to my surprise, stretched across and opened the driver's door from the inside.

"'Well, my door's broken,' she told me with a laugh. I don't know if she's fixed it yet or not. This tells me something about her being unpretentious; you would think she's got people waiting on her hand and foot, but she doesn't. Maybe she doesn't want it. She's pretty independent."[25]

When Laura returned to Midland for her father's funeral, she once again was brought back to the church in which she had spent much of her youth. She had been baptized at First United Methodist and sang in the children's choir.

She had also attended Sunday school in the education wing.

She had been married in this church, and rejoined the congregation with her own family until she and George moved from Midland in 1981. Now, she was honoring the man who had helped her grow up safe and strong, in a world of sweetness and innocence that would forever linger as a warm, reassuring memory.

Midland has come to represent "hometown" for both Laura and George. Although Laura had a three-year head start over George when it came to growing up there, they have nine childhood years in common that shaped their perspective of the world. In Midland, they shared an upbringing by parents who found strength in the church, another factor that caused each of them to develop the strong faith that they share today.

"I was lucky to have loving parents who made me feel secure," Laura told Oprah in an interview for her magazine in May 2001, "and that has certainly been a huge advantage. I also have faith in God. I truly think life is a gift, and everything in the world is a gift to all of us."[26]

George shared his feelings about his hometown in a letter

to the Midland County Historical Society upon the publication of their book, *Historic Midland*, in 1998: "To me, Midland means friends and family. There is no better place to have grown up. . . . I remember neighbors worrying about neighbors. I remember Church and backyard barbecues. . . . My roots are there, my friends are there, and many of my beliefs are rooted in the philosophy that embodies Midland."[27]

Laura has expressed her love and respect for her West Texas home turf in many ways, including a written piece that is beloved by Texans. All of the reading she has done throughout her life has impacted upon her writing, as evidenced in a lyrical piece she wrote for a book containing photographs and poetry of West Texas.

In her foreword to *Whatever the Wind Delivers: Celebrating West Texas and the Near Southwest*, she describes the region with a nature writer's grace:

> To survive, every day is a negotiation, an agreement, an acceptance of terms that the soil and the sky outline without the slightest bit of consideration. And yet, even at its worst—at its dustiest, hottest, and driest—the region is rich with anticipation and hope for a merciful change. And it does change.
>
> Just when a man resigns his fields to a dry season, precious rain bursts from a cloud, calming the dust about his boots, washing the red dirt off the windows of his pickup and summoning birds to bathe and drink.
>
> This is the paradox of West Texas and the mighty Southwest. It is at once dull and unpredictable; subtle and grand.[28]

CHAPTER 2

Laura Welch:
Teacher and Librarian

"Teachers have a more profound impact on our society and culture than any other profession."
—LAURA BUSH

"Most people don't know anything about me, but based on the things that have been published, people probably think I'm a shy librarian. . . . Well, very few librarians fit the stereotype: They're people who like knowledge and are interested in a lot of different things."
—LAURA BUSH[1]

"THE POET JOHN KEATS ONCE said that childhood should be full of sweet dreams and health and quiet breathing," Laura Bush recalled in a speech to the National Federation of Republican Women in August 2000. "I was blessed to know such a childhood. Some of my fondest memories are of sitting with my mother's arm around me, listening to her read. Little did I know that she was doing much more than providing comfort and entertainment. She was paving the way for learning and for success."[2]

When she became a teenager, Laura and her mother would read in the car during the 307-mile drive to Laura's grandparents' home in El Paso. "As she got older, we read regular novels," said Jenna Welch. "If we were driving out to El Paso, we would take turns driving and reading to each other."[3]

They clocked countless hours on the road together on those drives, as well as on trips to Laura's other grandparents in Lubbock, 120 miles north of Midland. Wide open spaces; long, relaxing drives; listening to her mother's voice and sharing her love for the written word—these experiences helped shape Laura's appreciation for nature as well as for literature.

"I remember riding to Lubbock nearly every other weekend to visit my grandmother," she once wrote. "The drive between Midland and Lubbock was beautiful to me as a child and even more beautiful to me as an adult because of the memories it evoked."[4]

There was never any question in the Welch household that Laura would go to college. Harold Welch had attended Texas Tech in Lubbock but did not earn a degree, and he was determined that his daughter would have the opportunity to go to college when the time came.

He began saving for Laura's college education when she was very young. "My father took out an education policy for me when I was in the first grade, and he used to say, 'You're going to college.' My parents taught me the importance of a strong faith, and they instilled in me a passion for learning and doing my best. They had high expectations."[5]

Not only did Laura know by the second grade that she wanted to go to college to become a teacher, but in her first year of junior high, she knew exactly which college she wanted to attend. Not surprisingly, it was a book that helped her make up her mind.

"When I was in the seventh grade, I read a biography of Doak Walker," she said. "From that point forward, I wanted to attend SMU."[6] The book was entitled *Doak Walker: Three-Time All-American*, written by one of Walker's professors at Southern Methodist University, Dorothy Kendall Bracken.

Walker was a football legend who played at SMU in the

late 1940s. He earned All-American honors in 1947, 1948, and 1949, and was dubbed "the Golden Boy of the Southwest Conference," "the Doaker," and "Mr. Football." As a junior in 1948, he won the Heisman Trophy—the only SMU player ever to do so. Walker was a versatile player, playing running back, wide receiver, quarterback, and defensive in college as well as in his six seasons as a professional with the Detroit Lions.

One journalist described Walker as a "beautiful, All-American gridiron boy," and his modesty and all-around niceness were as legendary as his athletic skills.

"People had more than respect for Doak," said Joe Schmidt, a former Detroit Lions captain and coach. "It was more like adoration. You could never find anything bad to say about the guy. . . . If modern-day guys need anybody to look at, if anyone should be a role model to plan their life after, he certainly would be an example."[7]

For Texans like Laura, curiosity and admiration were mixed with pride. She wanted to attend the institution that had brought out the best in Doak Walker. Maybe it would bring out the best in her.

Laura has often referred to teaching as a "calling." She was drawn to this profession while also recognizing that it was a traditional career route for women when she started college in 1964. "At one point in our country's history, high-achieving women usually chose teaching as a career," Laura said in the *Oprah* magazine interview. "Now high-achieving women can choose anything."[8]

Only after graduating from SMU in 1968, when feminism was in full swing did Laura briefly question her choice of career. One day, she brought up the issue with her father, telling him that she felt he had limited her by "programming" her to become a teacher when she could have entered any number of other professions, such as law.

But Harold Welch was not a chauvinist; in fact, his response revealed that he would have unhesitatingly supported Laura in any career decision. After Laura's comment, her father "almost immediately pulled out his wallet," she recalled, "and said, 'I'll send you to law school.' He would have loved to. But, I had to admit, when he did that, that I didn't want to be a lawyer. I wanted to be a teacher."[9]

Laura's teacher training began freshman year at SMU in the fall of 1964. Southern Methodist University in Dallas was somehow isolated from the anti-war movement that rocked campuses at Berkeley, Chicago, New Haven, New York, and other cities. Unlike the other schools, SMU did not hold rallies against President Lyndon Johnson as he increased the number of U.S. troops in South Vietnam from 20,000 to over 500,000 during Laura's undergraduate years.

Talk about the war was done in private, among her Kappa Alpha Theta sorority sisters and friends like Polly Chappell Davis, one of four pals from Midland who went to SMU at the time.

The rebellious heyday of the 1960s passed by SMU, which retained the conservative aura of the 1950s during Laura's stay. Founded in 1911, SMU is a conservative, private university set in the upscale University Park section of Dallas. The area around the campus is dotted with parks, crossed with tree-lined streets and luxury homes. Although it lies within the Dallas city limits, University Park is a town unto itself with its own fire and police departments. In the 1960s, the four-square-mile enclave of University Park—including SMU—was as removed from the racial unrest in Dallas's downtown neighborhoods as it was from the antiwar protests in California and New York.

SMU was not a wild place, and the most outrageous thing Laura did was continue to smoke cigarettes, a habit she started in high school—and which she has since quit.

"My generation was just right on the cusp," said Laura. "When I started at SMU, girls still wore dresses to school the whole time. . . . It was a fairly conservative campus compared with how it was just a few years after that for the little brothers and sisters of my friends. Even growing up in Midland, they had a different experience than we did. So we weren't wild like that. I mean, people smoked cigarettes—and I did. And they drank beer, and that was sort of the way college kids were wild when I was there."[10]

One of Laura's favorite pastimes was playing bridge, and her friend Peggy Weiss recalled that "in college we used to sit out by my swimming pool and play bridge and smoke and drink Coke. Laura was excellent at bridge." They also listened to records—Laura had a huge collection that she had brought from home—and the highlight of their freshman year was listening to the Beatles' newly released first album, *Meet the Beatles*.

"We played that album over and over again," said Peggy. "Regan liked Paul, I liked John, and I think Laura liked all of them."[11] Like millions of others, Laura will always connect where she was in 1964 with "I Want to Hold Your Hand," "Till There Was You" and "All My Loving."

Sometimes the mothers of the four Midland friends would come to Dallas to spend time with their daughters. "There were four of us that went to SMU," said Lucy McFarland Woodside, "and all of our mothers were friends. . . . They would do a 'girls trip' to come into Dallas to shop and see us. We always enjoyed it because it was fun getting the girls and the mothers together."[12]

SMU was as positive an experience as Laura had hoped. Her courses were stimulating, her grades at SMU were excellent, and she was popular with both sexes.

"Her friends noticed that she had a polished reserve," wrote George W. Bush biographer Bill Minutaglio, "a way of easily letting others lead the conversation. Laura Welch was content, they said, to listen—and listen attentively, a fact that would reveal itself when she would mention something someone else had said months before."[13]

She was also funny, according to friends like sorority sister Susan Nowlin. "Her room was always the central headquarters for fun. . . . One day Laura says, 'I need to practice my Miss America wave.' We all started laughing and asked her what she was talking about. She laughed and said, 'You just never know when it will come in handy.' She put her hand up in the air, middle fingers together and moving it in a mechanical motion. Now when we see her on television before she gets into a car or as she walks to the stage, we'll scream, 'Look! She's doing her Miss America wave!'"[14]

Laura majored in elementary education, and her sixty-six-semester-hour education degree program included courses in Child Growth and Development, Teaching of Reading in the Elementary School, Children's Literature, the Child in the Elementary School, and orientation courses for teaching math, social studies, science, and the language arts.

After graduating from SMU in 1968, Laura took a holiday

in Europe with her aunt, uncle, and cousin from Dallas. "Laura's uncle, Dr. Mark Welch, is a surgeon in Dallas," said Laura's mother. "He had booked a two-week medical conference trip to several countries in Europe and invited his wife and daughter and Laura along. Originally Laura told us she wanted to go with a group of girls from college on a European camping trip, but we weren't sure about that; we were pretty protective. But then this chance came along and she wanted to go. Her cousin, Mary Welch, is about five years younger, and the two girls were roommates during the trip."

Before leaving on her trip, Laura applied for a job with the Dallas Public Schools. She was disappointed to find that there were no openings in the school system when she returned from Europe, so she took a job in an insurance office. A few months later, she got a call from the Dallas school system. There was an opening, and Laura took the job. She taught the third grade in Dallas for almost a year.

Laura's next teaching job was in Houston. The second classroom of students to address her as "Miss Welch" was a group of second-graders at John F. Kennedy Elementary, a predominantly black school. Most of the students lived in the Independence Heights neighborhood in the northern section of Houston.

Times were changing for the neighborhood; following the enactment of President Johnson's Voting Rights Act of 1965, black voting increased in Houston and black residents began getting elected to the state legislature and other political offices. In 1971, Judson Robinson became the first African American to be elected to the Houston City Council in almost 100 years.

"I particularly wanted to teach in a minority school," Laura said. "This was a mainly African-American student population at JFK Elementary and I loved it. I think mainly I just learned about the dignity of every human and every child, and how important every single child is and how important each one of their lives are."[15]

Laura took to the job, and the children took to their teacher. "The kids really did love her," said Larry Gatson, one of her second-grade students. "If you had problems with reading and spelling, she'd take a little more time with you."[16]

In fact, Laura became so attached to her class that she asked to move with her students to the third grade the following year.

During her years at JFK Elementary, Laura lived in Houston's most popular "singles" apartment complex, Chateaux Dijon, at 16201 El Camino Real. These apartments, built in 1963, were premier luxury units featuring tall, narrow-angled roofs and round towers in the style of a sixteenth-century French chateau—mixed with simple modern lines of the '60s.

Unknown to Laura, George W. Bush lived on the opposite end of the sprawling complex, the rowdier side. "In an odd coincidence of fate," he wrote in his autobiography, "we lived in the same apartment complex in Houston . . . she lived on the quiet side of Chateaux Dijon; I lived on the loud side, where we played volleyball in the pool until late at night. . . . Our paths never crossed."[17]

George was a pilot in the Texas Air National Guard and moved to the Chateaux in the summer of 1970, living alone in a one-bedroom apartment. Laura shared a place with her friend Jan Donnelly O'Neill from Midland. While George partied with his friends and drove around Houston in his blue Triumph convertible, Laura kept a low profile and went to bed early on school nights.

After two years at the Houston school, Laura reflected on what she liked best about her job. English classes had been her favorites in college, and she loved teaching reading best of all, so at the end of the 1969 school year she decided to specialize and become a school librarian.

In 1970 she enrolled in the Library Science graduate program at the University of Texas in Austin.

When Laura enrolled in the graduate program, tuition and fees for one semester, or "long session," totaled about $200.00. Since then, college costs everywhere have increased drastically, and today tuition for one semester *hour* at the graduate school is $120.00.

A statement in the admissions section from the 1969–1971 Graduate School of Library Science Catalog sheds light on the fact that these were the days before equal opportunity: "All applicants . . . will be considered on the basis of personality, alertness, state of health, freedom from physical handicaps, and age."

Laura's two-year master's program required thirty-six semester hours of classes, all of which these were held in Main, the central building on campus that includes the 307-foot University of Texas Tower.

Courses in Laura's master's program included Children's Literature, School Libraries, Literature for Adolescents, Library Materials, Cataloging and Classification, and Library Administration. One course, Technical Services, included the topics entitled "Introductory Computer Based Retrieval" and "Experimental Automatic Documentation," subjects that hinted at the high-tech information services age to come. This degree gave

Laura professional training in her favorite area, children's reading, as she worked through classes that taught how to evaluate books for children, offer reading guidance, and develop a lasting interest in reading. The degree also involved learning about the history of libraries and information systems in various civilizations, understanding the role of books and libraries in today's society, and, of course, the principles of cataloging and classification.

Laura graduated with a Master of Library Science degree in 1972. "We're extremely proud of her," said Mary Lynne Rice-Lively, Ph.D., Assistant Dean of the Graduate School of Library and Information Science, Laura's alma mater. "As a library professional, it's great to have such a high-profile person tell the story of library and information services. We make fun of ourselves a lot, but it's actually a very service-oriented profession. Many people are drawn to our field because of the service aspect of it."

Twenty-nine years later, when her husband was sworn in as president, Laura became only the second First Lady to possess an advanced college degree. The first was her predecessor, Hillary Rodham Clinton, who has a law degree.

The year following Laura's graduation she moved back to Houston, where she had begun her teaching career, and took her first job as a public librarian. She was hired as the children's librarian at the McCrane-Kashmere Gardens Library on Pardee Street.

One of the reasons Laura wanted to work in downtown Houston was to enter a bigger singles scene. "I didn't have the opportunity to meet that many men to date," she said, "and I thought by working in a big public library in downtown

Houston, I might have a different social life."[18] She went out with a few men, but no one special came into her life.

After a year in Houston, Laura moved back to Austin and returned to the elementary school setting she loved. She became a school librarian at Mollie Dawson School, a minority elementary school like JFK Elementary in Houston. Dawson, located on 3001 South 1st Street, had a primarily Hispanic population of students who lived on the south side of Austin. Laura was at home with Spanish, which she had studied in high school— including the summer trip to Monterrey, Mexico.

As a school librarian, helping students learn how to research and become lifelong learners, Laura had found the perfect job that combined her love for books with her passion for teaching. Austin felt like home, and by the summer of 1977, at age thirty, she had settled happily into her career. Many weekends she made the 490-mile drive to Midland to visit her parents and her friends, and in the summer of her thirtieth year she made a trip home that would change everything. At a backyard barbecue given by her now-married former roommate, Jan Donnelly O'Neill, she was introduced to Midland's most eligible bachelor—a good-looking ex–National Guard pilot named George W. Bush.

CHAPTER 3

George W.: Fighter Pilot and Oil Man

"Bush was a smart, hard-working Texas oil man who paid his own dues."
—THE MIDLAND REPORTER-TELEGRAM

"A PRODUCT OF THE MIDLAND SCHOOL system, once a tobacco-chewing oilman with only one suit and a ten-year-old station wagon, the man who could be the next president of the United States is a curious mix of Ivy Leaguer and good ol' boy," wrote John Paul Pitts in the *Midland Reporter-Telegram* during the presidential campaign of 2000.

George W. was two years old when his parents moved from New Haven, Connecticut to Midland, and he lived there until he was thirteen. "It was a happy childhood," he wrote in his autobiography. "Midland was a small town. . . . No one locked their doors, because you could trust your friends and neighbors. I was surrounded by love and friends and sports."[1]

His father, George Herbert Walker Bush, had moved to West Texas in 1948 just after graduating from Yale. George the elder was born and raised in Massachusetts, where he attended Phillips Academy. On graduation day, at age eighteen, he enlisted and became the youngest pilot in the U.S. Navy after earning his wings the following year.

George Bush flew torpedo bombers in the Pacific for three years. Then, on September 2, 1944, his plane was hit by anti-aircraft fire during a bombing run over one of the Japanese-occupied islands of Chichi Jima. Bush's plane caught fire, but he was still able to hit his targets before bailing out over the ocean. Unfortunately, his two crewmates were killed. Bush, however, was rescued at sea by a Navy submarine and was awarded three Air Medals and the Distinguished Flying Cross for his service in the Navy.

After the war, Bush enrolled at Yale University and earned a degree in economics. He was captain of the baseball team, member of the honor society Phi Beta Kappa, president of his fraternity, and, like his father before him, a member of the secret Skull & Bones society. After graduating, he immediately followed the opportunity trail to West Texas, where many uprooted Northerners and Easterners were making a start in the oil business.

"Former President George H. W. Bush didn't want an easy life handed to him," states his biography in the *Permian Basin Petroleum Hall of Fame.* "Bush needed challenges that living on the Eastern Seaboard couldn't provide, so he made his own way and started in the oil patch."[2]

Midland was growing rapidly and, in 1950, housed the offices of more than 200 oil companies. Bush began in the sales end of the business, selling oil equipment supplies for International Derrick and Equipment Co. He then cofounded a small company that dealt with oil royalties.

In 1953, he cofounded Zapata Petroleum Corporation and achieved the dream of every wildcatter since the 1920s—of the 137 wells drilled in the company's Jameson field, not one came up dry. In 1954, he became cofounder and president of Zapata Off-Shore. Bush was financially secure and only thirty-five years old when he resettled his family to Houston to run Zapata in 1959. He then decided to enter politics.

George Herbert Walker Bush's father, Prescott Bush, was the first Bush elected to office. He was a partner in a Wall Street investment firm and served as a U.S. senator from Connecticut from 1952 to 1962. Prescott's wife, Dorothy Walker, was the daughter of another Wall Street scion, George Herbert Walker, a power broker in banking, politics, and sports (the prestigious golf event, the Walker Cup, is named after the family).

His namesake, George H. W. Bush, became a member of the U.S. House of Representatives, ambassador to the United Nations, chairman of the Republican National Committee, chief of the U.S. liaison office in China, director of the Central Intelligence Agency (CIA), vice president, and president.

During leave from the Navy in 1945, George H. W. married Barbara Pierce. A native of Rye, New York, Barbara brought with her an impressive lineage: She is a great-great-great niece of Franklin Pierce, the fourteenth President of the United States, and her father, Marvin Pierce, was the publisher of the enduring *McCall's* and *Redbook* magazines.

She had met George, whom everyone called "Poppy," when she was sixteen years old and in preparatory school, and agreed to be his senior prom date at Andover. They made an appealing couple—intelligent, enthusiastic, and even then, devoted to their country.

Just before starting at Smith, Barbara worked for the summer at a "nuts and bolts" factory to help the war effort. Once on campus, she, like her daughter-in-law to be, showed a talent for sports, becoming captain of the girls' soccer team her freshman year. It was to be a special year for Barbara: That Christmas she and George announced their engagement.

Barbara dropped out of Smith during her sophomore year to get married. The ceremony was held on January 6, 1945, in the First Presbyterian Church in Rye. They honeymooned in Sea Island, Georgia, and then began a migration from one air base to another as the Navy sent George to new locations.

Barbara staunchly supported her husband, but was fearful that George would be sent back to the Pacific Theater.

"By now I realized that what my dad had told me before I married was true," she wrote in her memoir. "He said that every day you stay married, you fall more and more in love with your husband or wife. It was certainly true in my case, and I did not want George to return to the war."[3]

Happily, he was not sent back, and at the end of the war they moved to New Haven, Connecticut where George attended Yale.

George H. W. and Barbara Bush went on to have six children. Tragically, their daughter, Robin, died of leukemia at age three. Surviving were George W., Jeb, Marvin, Neil, and Dorothy.

Because he left his Connecticut birthplace when he was a baby, George W. has always considered Midland, Texas his hometown. He played Little League baseball in the hot, dry wind, watched tumbleweed roll down the street, and wiped the dust from his desk at school every morning.

"We moved there in the midst of a long drought," he wrote. "I remember giant sandstorms blowing in. You could look out the back window but not see the fence because the sand was blowing so thick and hard."[4]

Baseball became one of the loves of his life. "He basically was just a baseball-playing Bush boy," recalled one of his friends from Midland. "He played baseball all the time. He was just a typical, everyday kid."[5]

On Sundays he went to the First Presbyterian Church—where his father was an elder and both of his parents taught

Sunday school—and on weekdays he attended Sam Houston Elementary.

George's childhood Midland home at 1412 West Ohio is currently being transformed into the George W. Bush Childhood Home Museum. A brainchild of the Midland Board of Realtors, the project includes refurbishing the home with vintage furniture and other items from the 1951 to 1955 period, when George lived in the house. The site will also include a welcoming center and a separate museum and exhibit center about the Bush family. George mentioned the house when he returned to Midland for a victory celebration after the presidential election of 2000.

"It seems improbable now," he said in his speech in the center of town, "but in that little house on Ohio Street, right down the road from here, it was hard to envision then the future of two presidents and a governor of Florida. There's so much optimism in this place, such a passion for the possible. You see it everywhere in Midland and you see it throughout West Texas and I certainly saw it in the home where I was raised."

Between the seventh and eighth grades, the family moved to Houston, where George's father had moved the headquarters of his oil company. Instead of enrolling in the public junior high, George attended Kinkaid, a private school, for two years. His family switched to the Episcopal Church, which was his father's denomination, and George was fascinated with the formal ritual that was absent in the Presbyterian Church. He served communion during the early service and, as a teenager, began to seriously think about his faith.

After finishing his junior high years, George went away to boarding school at Phillips Academy in Andover, Massachusetts, where his father had gone. "Andover was a family tradition; my parents wanted me to learn not only the academics but also how to thrive on my own," he wrote.[6] After graduating from Phillips he followed family tradition once again and entered Yale University. George majored in history and described his college years as "a time of hard work during the week and parties on the weekend."

He was a cheerleader, a member of the Delta Kappa Epsilon fraternity, and was invited into a select on-campus society—one which his father and grandfather had also joined in their day. "My senior year I joined Skull and Bones," he wrote, "a secret society, so secret I can't say anything more."[7] Each year, fifteen juniors are chosen for the society and after initiation become members in their senior year.

"The Bonesmen met in a triple-padlocked, windowless mausoleum on High Street," wrote Bill Minutaglio in *First Son*, "that was filled with the same sorts of burnished knickknacks, skulls . . . and worn leather chairs found in the old societies and clubs at English universities."[8]

In his junior year at Yale, Bush decided to get engaged to his girlfriend back home in Houston. The relationship didn't survive the long distance and infrequent meetings, however, and the couple finally broke their engagement.

That left George free to pursue service to his country during the Vietnam War. While at Yale, he, like his fellow students, thought often of this war; everyone knew someone who had died and seniors were forced to decide how they would deal with military service after graduation. As soon as he graduated in 1968, George joined the Texas Air National Guard and started basic training at Lackland Air Base in San Antonio, Texas.

"There was no question in my mind that I was going to serve—I was going to go to the military in 1968," Bush said. "The question was, for me, what branch and when and how. And one of the things I made up my mind is I wanted to fly airplanes."[9]

His father's heroic World War II record played a large role in his decision. "I'm sure my dad's being a pilot influenced my decision," he wrote in *A Charge to Keep*. George's first pilot training took place at Moody Air Force Base in Valdosta, Georgia, where he learned to fly the T-41, T-37, and T-38 jets. After fifty-five weeks of training, he graduated from Moody and set out for Ellington Air Force Base in Houston. There he learned how to pilot the F-102A Delta Dagger Interceptor, a single-engine fighter jet.

"He played the role of fighter jock with considerable swagger," wrote Kenneth T. Walsh in *U.S. News & World Report*, "tucking a rakish orange scarf into his green flight suit, keeping his hair short and his shoes spit-shined. Always ready with a wisecrack and a smirk, the young lieutenant didn't take himself very seriously, even though his friends and superiors in the Guard said he was an excellent flier."[10]

George tried to participate in "Palace Alert," a program that sent National Guard flyers to Vietnam to relieve active-duty pilots, but his commanding officer turned him down. He cited two reasons: first, he had not logged enough flying hours to qualify for the unit; second, the program was being phased out. George remained on active duty with the Guard until 1973, working a variety of jobs in Houston at the same time and living the bachelor life at the Chateaux Dijon.

He admittedly defines those years as "nomadic," and one of his fellow pilots summarized George's world in those free-wheeling days: "He was a good-looking first lieutenant-bachelor-fighter pilot. Just think of the environment."[11]

George was on the road continually in Texas in 1970, making speeches and helping out with his father's Senate campaign. Although George H. W. had two congressional terms behind him, he ended up losing to Democrat Lloyd Bentsen.

During the campaign, George W. met John White, a former football pro with the Houston Oilers who had launched a program called Project PULL—Professional United Leadership League—in Houston. This inner-city program provided mentoring and many other services to poor children from Houston's poverty-stricken south side.

White brought in famous baseball, football, and basketball stars to give motivational talks to the kids, and the center was a safe haven where the kids could play pool and board games. They could also have a snack and talk to staff members or volunteers about what was going on in their lives.

George worked full-time at PULL for nine months, both in the center and out in the wealthy neighborhoods of Houston raising money for the organization. "He was instrumental in connecting a lot of the upper-class and well-to-do people with the program," said Edgar Arnold, a PULL staffer.[12]

George visited Houston's wealthy residents in their homes and offices, delivering a lively pitch about PULL and the important work it was doing. People responded to the son of the congressman, and he was able to raise awareness about PULL in the population that could give it the most financial support.

At the center, he was often the only white person on staff. He sometimes took the kids on field trips to juvenile prisons to show them the cost of crime and, one day, brought a group of them to the airport and gave them their first airplane ride.

"My job gave me a glimpse of a world I had never seen," wrote George. "It was tragic, heartbreaking, and uplifting, all at the same time. I saw a lot of poverty . . . [and] I saw good and decent people working to try to help lift these kids out of their terrible circumstances."[13]

Meanwhile, as George was learning about minorities and poverty at PULL, Laura was also working with children on the other side of town at the McCrane-Kashmere Gardens Library. Ironically, both George and Laura had full-time jobs with children and saw many of the same ones from week to week.

Among George's "regulars" was a six-year-old boy named Jimmy who became, in George's words, "like a little brother." He came to the center every day and never left George's side. When he came in barefoot one day, George took him out and bought him a pair of shoes. Like all the kids at the center, Jimmy was poor and troubled and tough. George witnessed the boy's home situation first-hand when he took him home one night. The house, from the rotting porch to the broken door, was falling apart and loud music was blaring inside. When Jimmy's mother opened the door, George could tell she was on drugs, and his heart broke even more.

"Jimmy was happy to be home," he wrote in *A Charge to Keep,* "but I was incredibly sad to leave him there." When he returned to PULL years later to speak at John White's memorial service, he learned to his great sorrow that Jimmy had been shot and killed.

George finished his service duty with the Texas Air National Guard, quit his job at PULL, and moved to Cambridge, Massachusetts in 1973 to enroll in the MBA program at Harvard Business School. In this rigorous setting, he faced the combined pressures of a heavy academic load, anti-Republican/anti-Nixon sentiment raging in Harvard Square, and the ever-present Bush-Walker legacy of extraordinary accomplishment.

In his biography of George W., Bill Minutaglio stated that George often spent time with his family on the East Coast while at Harvard. It was here that George began to develop a sharp focus for the first time in his life. He looked forward to visits by one of his favorite cousins, Elsie Walker, who understood the psychological pressures of being in that family.

"He was working hard," she told Minutaglio. "This is not an easy family to grow up in. All of us had to come to grips with the fact that there are enormously successful people in it and a lot of pressure to succeed."[14]

George graduated from Harvard in June 1975, and moved to Midland to start out in the oil business, as his father had more than twenty-five years earlier. The elder Bush had been the first Easterner to make a million dollars in the 1950s oil boom, and did it before the age of thirty-five.

A new oil boom had hit the Permian Basin in the 1970s and the town was bursting with another wave of growth. So many people flocked to the town that some newcomers had no housing. "We had people living in tents all down the Interstate because there were not enough apartments," recalled Todd Houck.

George did find an apartment, however, and went to work as a landman, learning the process of buying and selling oil and gas leases.

The oil industry boom of the 1970s was triggered by the OPEC oil embargo of 1973. In October of that year, Arab members of the Organization of the Petroleum Exporting Countries

(Iran, Iraq, Kuwait, Saudi Arabia, Venezuela, and six other countries) punished the United States for its support of Israel in the Yom Kippur War, which erupted on October 5. OPEC decreased its exports, which resulted in a drastic cut in the U.S. oil supply with a simultaneous rise in the price of crude oil. Supply dropped but demand among U.S. consumers did not, and the price of oil and gasoline remained high.

President Richard Nixon called upon citizens to conserve, gas stations voluntarily closed on Sundays to save fuel, long lines formed at the pumps the rest of the week, highway speeds were lowered, and the nation fell into an "energy crisis." U.S. oil companies stepped up production and exploration, and in April 1974, construction began on the Trans-Alaskan Pipeline. This 800-mile system would bring oil from large reserves at Prudhoe Bay to awaiting ships at Valdez in the Pacific.

The sudden need for more domestic supplies brought the oil industry back into full swing in Texas. George's friends in Midland had told him about the exciting potential in the oil business while he was still at Harvard, and he started in the business by working as a landman for various companies.

"It was the time for reinvestment in the oil industry," said oilman and longtime friend Joseph I. O'Neill III, "and there were twelve or so of us who all moved back out here at the same time."[15] Between 1973 and 1981, the price of oil increased by 800 percent, and Midland cashed in on this boom as the business center of the Permian Basin oil industry.

In his first job as a landman, George secured leases of land that gave oil companies the rights to drill. This entailed research at the courthouse, digging up files that reported who owned the mineral rights (oil, gas, and uranium) to the land that the oil company was interested in. The owner of the land, such as a rancher, holds the surface rights but not necessarily the mineral rights of the property. Surface rights consist of the land on the surface down to the center of the earth—an entire slice of the planet—but not its mineral resources. When a well hits, the owner of the mineral rights get a royalty from the production of any oil or gas that is produced.

George's work as a landman taught him many of the fundamentals of the oil and gas industry and forged friendships with oil executives. "George did a little bit of everything," said F. H. "Buzz" Mills Jr., who shared an office with him on the fourth floor of the Midland National Bank Building. "We would sometimes discuss what we were doing, but George didn't need a lot of help. With his dad's background, he knew something about the oil business, and in Midland all of his friends, or most of them, had been in the oil business."[16]

George began to trade mineral and royalty interests and formed his own company, Arbusto (Spanish for *Bush*) Energy, in 1978. The company expanded its operations to become Bush Exploration, but it did not uncover profitable wells. To save the business, in 1982 George merged with another small Midland oil company, Spectrum 7. Spectrum was owned by Mercer Reynolds and William DeWitt, whose family once owned the Cincinnati Reds baseball team. George and his two new partners would later buy the Texas Rangers baseball team together.

The risks of oil exploration in the Permian Basin are high, as shown in an eye-opening exhibit in Midland's Petroleum Museum. The chances of finding a very small oil field are 1 in 15, a small field 1 in 50, a medium field 1 in 200, and a big oil field 1 in 1,000. In 1984, when George became chairman of

Spectrum 7, he made frequent trips to the Northeast to find investors who would spread out the risk and fund the company's 180 wells. But in the mid-1980s the boom ended, abruptly, in the wake of new moves from OPEC. (By this time George's father was in the White House as vice-president—he would be elected president in 1988.)

"OPEC flooded the market with cheaper oil and drove the price down," said Todd Houck of Midland's Petroleum Museum. "If it cost you eight dollars to bring a barrel of oil to the surface and you're only going to sell it for ten, you're going to lose money. There were death throes for about two or three years here. When the price of oil started dropping in the 1980s it caused a lot of people a lot of heartache around here."[17]

George saw his company fail practically overnight, along with three Midland banks and many other oil companies. "Drilling stopped," he wrote. "Midland was suffering through its version of the stock market crash of 1929."[18]

Spectrum 7 was sold to Harken Energy in 1986, and George joined the board of directors and worked as a consultant for the company. He received hundreds of thousands of shares of Harken stock in the deal, two-thirds of which he sold in 1990 for approximately $850,000.

Prescott Bush and George Herbert Walker Bush both made their fortunes before turning to politics, but George W.'s trajectory veered away somewhat from that path. He ran for office for the first time in 1977 as a fledgling oilman, then awaited his next political opportunity while working as managing general partner of the Texas Rangers.

In each political campaign, George has had to fight the stereotype of the Ivy-league Easterner, an outsider lured to

Texas's oil industry—the same carpetbagger image that had plagued his father throughout his career. But those who worked with him in Midland are fiercely protective of George's Texas identity and proud of his business ethics.

"Around Midland it is hard to find anyone, among those who knew him, who will say anything except that Bush was a smart, hard-working Texas oilman, who paid his own dues," wrote the *Midland Reporter-Telegram.* "Bush may have had the privilege of a New England breeding and education, but his ways and his values are pure Texas."

Jim McAnnich, one of George's first employees at Arbusto, recalled, "George was a bona fide oilman. He didn't make it by being the vice president's son."[19]

Before tying up his deal with Harken, George made sure that all of his Spectrum 7 employees had a new job. This demonstration of loyalty made a deep impression on the community. "When he left Midland," said Todd Houck, "he made sure that every single one of his employees got a job. I can point to ten people in the oil business who are successful, but they're also cutthroat. They can structure deals where if the well comes in they make money, but if it doesn't, they don't lose money—but all their investors do. George W. didn't structure his deals that way. If everybody lost, he lost, too."

When the bottom suddenly dropped out of the 1970s oil boom, Midlanders faced yet another round of changing fortunes. "Midland people are very tenacious," said Houck. "In spite of the adversities at the end of the boom with these big oil companies pulling out, many people just opted to stay."

❖ ❖ ❖

IN THE HISTORY of the United States, only two families have produced father and son presidents. John Adams, the nation's second president elected in 1796, was father to John Quincy Adams, who won his second attempt at the presidency in 1824.

With two terms as Governor of Texas followed by a successful bid for the presidency, George W. Bush fulfilled the expectations of his formidable family legacy. During the presidential campaign, Barbara Bush reflected on the public service aspect of running for political office that motivated both of her sons to become governors.

"I'm over-awed by both Jeb [Governor of Florida] and George, truthfully, running for public office," she said in a television interview in 1999. "Life's been good to them and they've worked very hard; they've worked their way up through the system and they want to give back. I honestly believe that, and their father believes that."[20]

Oprah interviewed George on her television show during the presidential campaign in the autumn of 2000. One viewer asked George what he considered the public's largest misconception of him. "Probably that I'm running on my daddy's name," he answered. "I've lived with this all my life. But I love my dad a lot; he gave me the great gift of unconditional love. It's allowed me to feel like I could dare to fail and I could dare to succeed."[21]

CHAPTER 4

Highway Honeymoon

*"We just loved her from the beginning.
I thought my brother was the luckiest man
in the world . . . Laura is the calm
amid George's storm."*
—DOROTHY BUSH
(George W.'s sister)

B Y THE MID-1970s, Laura's crowd of thirty-something hometown friends were all married. Among them was Laura's high school friend and college roommate, Jan Donnelly, who had married Joe O'Neill III in 1972. Joe's father was an ex-FBI agent from Philadelphia who had moved to Midland during the 1950s oil boom. The same boom had attracted George's father, and the two became close friends. Their sons, George W. and Joey, whom George called "Spider," were pals in elementary school and played on the same Little League team. Jan knew Laura, Joe knew George, and they both tried several times to get the two singles together.

In the back of her mind, Jan had her doubts about whether or not Laura and George would hit it off because their personalities were so completely different. Laura was reserved, calm, and patient, while George was gregarious and restless.

In astrology, the traits that have been described about Laura and George fall neatly into their sun sign profiles. Laura is a Scorpio: loyal, deep-thinking, intense, reclusive, honest, persistent, with a frank sense of humor. George is a Cancer: instinctual, sensitive, with a tough outer shell to protect a tender heart. Both were "water signs"—emotional, intense, and passionate about their beliefs.

Jan thought it was worth a try. After all, George was from one of America's most famous political families. He had been a dashing fighter pilot and, by some strange twist of fate, was now

Midland's most eligible bachelor. Laura, one of Jan's best friends, was the same age and still looking for Mr. Right.

Laura was working as a librarian at Mollie Dawson Elementary in Austin in 1977 and dating some of the capital city's high-achievers. According to her friend Pamela Nelson, Laura dated young men "who were really bright. She wouldn't waste her time with anyone who wasn't serious about their future."[1]

Nothing serious developed, however. Still, when Laura came home to visit her parents on weekends, she repeatedly turned down the O'Neills' entreaties to come over and meet their friend, George W. Bush. She just wasn't interested in pursuing Jan's invitation.

"She didn't want to turn a visit with her parents into an occasion for dating," recalled Jan. "But on one of those cool Midland nights, we said, 'Come on over and have hamburgers with us.' And she agreed."

Laura had held them off as long as possible, knowing that they were anxious about hooking her up. "I think our friends wanted to fix us up because we were literally the last two people [of all our friends who hadn't married]," laughed Laura.[2]

George had landed back in Midland two years before and was learning the ropes in the oil business. In July 1977, he also announced that he was running for the soon-to-be-vacant seat in the Nineteenth Congressional District. This was the main reason Laura kept politely refusing to meet him at the O'Neills'.

"I was so uninterested in politics," she said. "I thought he was someone real political, and I wasn't interested."[3]

But when they finally met that summer evening at the backyard cookout, something clicked. They talked nonstop and

George stayed until midnight—highly unusual for him, according to friends. Everyone, especially the O'Neills, knew that he went to bed early and got up early to run, usually putting in three miles every morning. He always left dinner parties by nine o'clock. The fact that George whiled away the hours with Laura was a red-flag signal to Joe and Jan that this was something special.

The next night the four of them got together again to play miniature golf.

"I thought he was very fun," recalled Laura. "I also thought he was really cute. . . . He's also slightly outrageous once in awhile . . . and I found that a lot of fun."[4]

George felt that their different personalities complemented each other perfectly. Laura was a great listener, and he was a great talker. For him, it was love at first sight.

"We both, very quickly, fell in love with each other," he wrote in his autobiography. Laura said, "I don't know that it was love at first sight, [but] it was pretty close."

Laura went back to Austin that Sunday night, and George went down to visit her there the following weekend. The next day, he was due in Maine for the annual Bush vacation at their summer home in Kennebunkport. "I went and stayed one day," he said, "then flew back to Austin to see Laura. That's when my mother said she knew I was smitten."[5]

After vacation, he returned to work in Midland but flew to Austin every weekend. "He was bouncing off the walls just to impress her," said Joe O'Neill.

One of the qualities that Laura came to love in those first weeks was George's infectious high spirits. Her father had affected people the same way. "Both my dad and George tried to make people feel good," she said. George made her laugh, and she gradually fell for him as hard as he fell for her. Soon, they knew they were ready to get married. Both of them viewed the speedy courtship as natural, after all, they were in love, so why wait?

In October 1977, George brought Laura to Houston to meet his family. George H. W. and Barbara had just returned from a trip to China and Tibet.

"The day after we got home from our China trip," wrote Barbara, "George W. came to Houston with a beautiful young woman and announced they were getting married." Laura handled the scrutiny of George's grandmother, the formidable matriarch Dorothy Walker Bush, with a comeback that pleasantly surprised everyone. They had been talking about sports, a major obsession and source of fierce competition in the clan for generations. Dorothy asked, "What do you do?" Laura knew that she was expected to say tennis or skiing or something daring and competitive. Instead, she replied, "I read."

Barbara Bush recalled the elderly woman's response: "Mrs. Bush darn near collapsed."

When George's brother, Jeb, first met Laura that day, he clowned around and dropped to one knee, asking if George had popped the question yet. Without flinching, she said, "As a matter of fact, he has, and I've accepted."[6]

"She's one of the more elegant human beings I've ever met, said George's brother, Marvin, recalling that first meeting. "The doors were always slamming, everybody was running around and playing sports in an extremely male-oriented family. . . she has an extremely gracious and gentle way about her that brings peace to a place that could otherwise be chaotic."[7]

In another interview he described her entry into the family "like Audrey Hepburn walking into the 'Animal House.' Here was this bright, cerebral, lovely human being—a very serene-type person—coming into this chaotic environment known as the Bush household."[8]

Barbara, who has become a close friend of Laura, wrote, "Laura is a very special person, and I always thought that being an only child with few cousins, she was amused by us."[9]

Soon after Laura met the Bush family, George returned to Midland and took Harold and Jenna Welch out to dinner to formally request their daughter's hand in marriage. They were delighted, and gave their blessing, so George and Laura set the date for early November, just a month away. Throughout the whirlwind courtship, Jenna feared that George's speedy tactics would drive Laura away. She remembered the string of boyfriends from SMU who had come on too strong too fast, and how Laura had always broken up with them.

But this time, everything was different. "It was almost like we'd known each other forever," said Laura. "We had so much of the same background."[10] The timing was right, and neither of them felt any need to wait.

"George and I both were at a stage where we wanted to get married. We were happy and grateful to find each other because both of us were ready to settle down and start a family."[11] Later, Laura would admit that getting married so quickly after meeting George was the most impulsive thing she had ever done in her life.

The first week of November, 1977, George's parents arrived in Midland and hosted a wedding rehearsal dinner at the Hilton hotel downtown. On November 5—one day after the bride's thirty-first birthday—George and Laura were married at the First United Methodist Church in Midland. The eleven o'clock ceremony was small and remarkably plain—no bridesmaids, no groomsmen or other attendants—and only seventy-five guests.

Even though they had had only one month to plan the wedding, it was an unusually simple one, considering the national stature of the groom's father. George H. W., recently the director of the CIA and currently chairman of the First National Bank of Houston, was already being tapped by the Republican Party as their man for the presidential election of 1980.

Money was certainly no object, as the Welches or the Bushes could have funded a lavish wedding with all the trimmings. And with Laura their only child, Harold and Jenna had waited for this proud moment for thirty-one years and would have given her any kind of wedding she wanted.

But, according to Laura's mother, Laura and George kept things simple because they wanted to celebrate their marriage with their closest friends, and because George was busy with his congressional campaign.

"It was a very simple wedding; that's what *they* wanted," said Jenna Welch. "It wasn't as if she were a young bride whose family wanted to dominate the wedding. The people who were there were very close to them. They wanted their friends, not their family's friends."

The Welches were not disappointed that they didn't get to invite their own friends and extended family. Nor were they upset that Laura didn't ask for a big, traditional wedding.

"I'm sure I thought about it," reflected Jenna, "but Laura never was one that wanted a big show. And George was running for office," Jenna continued. "He had already declared his candidacy, and he didn't want a big wedding. He was very positive that he just wanted family."

The Welch and Bush parents were asked to invite only one couple each. Laura avoided the traditional wedding gown and veil and opted for a simple cream-colored skirt and blouse with a spray of flowers at the waist. The wedding announcement in the *Midland Reporter-Telegram* described her ensemble in an announcement published the next day:

"The bride wore a street-length dress of candlelight crêpe de Chine. It was styled with a long sleeved, tucked blouson bodice and a pleated skirt. She had a corsage of white gardenias at the waistline."[12]

"George sent all of us beautiful gardenia corsages," Laura's mother recalled, "and when Laura got hers she tried it on her blouse and it didn't look right, so she pinned it on her waist and it looked very nice."

Laura wore her thick, shoulder-length hair loose in much the same way she wore it every day. The four ushers who escorted guests down the green-carpeted aisle were her cousin, Robert Lane Welch, and George's three brothers, Jeb, Neil, and Marvin.

The wedding was held in the chapel of the First United Methodist Church, a smaller room that is dwarfed by the main sanctuary but which, on its own, could stand up in size to any typical small-town church. There are thirteen pews on each side of the aisle, and the stone wall at the front of the church is cut majestically from floor to ceiling by a stunning, abstract stained-glass window. Small, jewel-like stained-glass windows dot another wall, and even in the brightest hour of the day the chapel is dim and intimate.

Reverend Jerry Wyatt, who performed the ceremony, recalled George's body language at a pivotal moment that morning: "As soon as Laura and her dad stepped into the aisle back there, he just grew a little bit, got a little straighter. . . . He was very pleased that he had probably slowed down long enough to let her catch him."[13]

After the ceremony, everyone drove over to the Racquet Club of Midland for the reception. There were other parties going on that afternoon, and at one point the sounds of a barbershop quartet seeped through the wall. George's father got up, walked next door, and invited the group over to entertain his party. The four male singers filled the room with tight harmonies that suddenly gave the luncheon the air of an old-fashioned ice cream social.

The newlyweds then left for a short honeymoon to Mexico. When they returned, Laura moved into George's large brick house on Golf Course Road, which he had bought earlier that year. It was still a bit of a bachelor-pad mess, both inside and out, and Laura commented that the weeds in the yard were as tall as she was. However, she didn't have a lot of time to whip things into shape. They almost immediately hit the campaign trail.

Laura worried that the stress of campaigning, coupled with the stress of being newlyweds, might be hard on two people who were still getting to know each other. Not only did she have no political experience, she had always considered herself a Democrat and was a newcomer to the GOP.

"I'm a Republican by marriage," she told one reporter in a much later campaign. But George recalls that it "was a wonderful way to spend our first year of marriage. We were united on a common mission; we spent lots of time together." They hired a driver and rode in George's white Oldsmobile Cutlass throughout the Midland-Odessa-Lubbock district. Sometimes they sat in the back of a pickup and waved at townspeople as they made their way to the place where George would give a speech.

Laura had asked her mother-in-law for advice before setting out on the campaign trail with George. Barbara, who had been through many campaigns in her thirty-two years of marriage to George H., gave her one strong piece of advice: "Don't ever criticize his speeches."

Laura tried to follow her suggestion through most of the campaign, but one evening, in the final weeks, she let down her guard. She and George were pulling up to the house after a long drive home from Lubbock. George sensed that his speech hadn't gone well that day, and all the way home he waited for Laura to cheer him up. She didn't, and when they reached the driveway, he finally broke the ice.

"I didn't do very well, did I?" he asked.

"No, it wasn't very good," she agreed. George was so shocked that he forgot what he was doing and drove straight into the garage wall.

Without any previous interest or experience in politics, Laura had no expectations about what it would be like to hit the road and help her new husband run for office. As they drove along Highways 385, 82, and 87 to Lubbock and Interstate 20 to Odessa, she found herself pleasantly surprised that it was fun to be on the road, to talk for hours and enjoy the scenery that was so familiar to both of them. She recalled spending countless happy hours doing the same thing with her parents when she was growing up.

Laura also got to see George's natural talent for working a crowd, a gift, she joked, that he did not display back home under normal circumstances. "It's a great way to spend a honeymoon. George was great. I always thought he said the right thing. I thought he did the right thing. And then, when he went back to work . . . and I stayed home, then I started thinking he was a klutz."[14]

During their courtship, Laura made it clear that she didn't want to become a public person and get up in front of the public to give speeches. She would, of course, be happy to be George's private confidante and to provide emotional support, but she could not live in the spotlight, nor would she speak for him in public. George was just fine with Laura's reticence to become a public figure.

He promised her that their common West Texas background would bond them to a future resonating with the values they both shared while growing up. He also promised Laura that she would love his family. And he promised that she would never have to make a speech.

George's promise about "no speeches" was left in the dust just two months after the couple were married when he asked her to make a speech for him on the courthouse steps in Muleshoe, Texas. Her first speech was a humbling experience that remains painfully clear in Laura's memory, bearing little resemblance to those that would later distinguish her as a sincere, confident speaker.

Laura had worked on the Muleshoe speech, but hadn't polished it or created a strong final statement, and was nervous and disappointed in herself for not being better prepared.

"He asked me to go speak for him," she told MSNBC's Matt Lauer in a television interview, "and I had a really great start to my speech, but I hadn't really gotten far enough to have a very good ending. So I stood up and gave my few—what I thought were really pretty good—lines at the start and then I had to mumble and sit down."[15]

However embarrassing, the event did not compel Laura to retreat from the public eye. Rather, she worked on her lines and improved her delivery with each appearance—throughout that unsuccessful campaign, on to George's subsequent victorious run for governor and finally to the biggest political arena of them all, the campaign for the presidency of the United States.

Public speaking was not a skill she had anticipated developing. As a teacher in her twenties, Laura had devoted herself to an audience of approximately thirty children in the classroom and was very comfortable there. But falling in love with George not only launched her into public life, it also shifted her role as an educator and librarian to one who would create far-reaching programs—both as First Lady of Texas, and subsequently throughout the country as First Lady of the United States.

Laura Bush, born in West Texas and a former schoolteacher and librarian, is, at first glance, a conservative and traditional woman. But those who know her well have always looked to the day when America would discover her strength, warmth, intelligence, and humor. Journalists who covered Laura as the First Lady of Texas became very aware that Laura Bush is hardly a shy, timid, reticent librarian with nothing to say.

"Her composure and her reserve in public," wrote Gregory Curtis in *Time* magazine, "have led some to speculate that behind the benign exterior lies a steely woman who, if things get out of hand, is going to be taking names. But that's not her at all . . . she's funny. She likes to kid and tease and make subtle, one-line comebacks."[16]

Curtis, who wrote about the Bushes for *Texas Monthly* for several years, added that she is certainly not dominated by her husband and does not cower in his shadow.

Or, as her friend Lynne Cheney once put it, "Laura Bush doesn't feel a need to be anybody but who she is."

CHAPTER 5
Family Life

"The baseball years were probably the most idyllic time of their married life."
—JENNA WELCH

L AURA WAS TO FIND THAT FAMILY LIFE would be inextricably mixed with George's political aspirations. Once he had won the Republican primary in June 1978, his campaign began to focus on beating Democratic State Senator Kent Hance.

But the playing field had changed: Now, for the first time, George faced a firing line of attacks about being an Ivy League elitist who had no real business in Texas politics—the same line that his father had confronted during his first senate campaign of 1964.

Hance's campaign also tossed out barbs about George's reputation as a hard-drinking frat boy. A few days before the election, a letter was sent out to "Christian voters" pointing out that the Bush campaign had placed an ad in a Texas Tech newspaper announcing that free beer would be on tap at a Bush rally. The writer questioned George's character for using alcohol to woo the college vote.

The Bush campaign could have fought back by advertising the fact that Hance actually owned property on which that bar, a popular hangout for Texas Tech students, was located. But George decided against it.

"Just an instinctive move," he said. "In retrospect, I probably should have counterattacked with, 'How hypocritical is this?'"

Instead, he chalked it up as his "first confrontation with

cheap-shot politics" and went back to work at his energy company.

Laura had quit working when she married George, and the first year of their marriage was almost entirely immersed in the congressional campaign. When it was finally over, she settled in to a quiet life of housework and community activities such as volunteering with Midland's Junior League. George began to work hard on developing his oil business. Life was good. But both Laura and George soon recognized that something was painfully missing.

"When George and I married, we wanted to have a lot of children—and then we didn't," she said. In late 1980, they decided to adopt a child, and paid a visit to the Gladney adoption home in Fort Worth.

Laura knew of the home because her parents had visited there on a similar mission after she was born and after her mother had had several miscarriages. George and Laura did all the paperwork, waited, and finally were given a date on which a Gladney representative would make a home visit.

But to their delight, in March 1981 Laura discovered she was pregnant. She and George decided to put their adoption plans on hold and see how the pregnancy developed.

It was not to be an easy one. Laura was thirty-five years old, and the first sonogram bore amazing news: She was carrying twins. The Bushes were overjoyed—until the doctor diagnosed that it was a high-risk pregnancy. He warned that Laura would have to be very careful, and she agreed to take no chances.

Laura stayed at home while George went to the family gathering in Kennebunkport that summer, but he was so concerned about her and the babies that he only stayed one day.

In September, nearing the end of her pregnancy, Laura's doctor ordered her confined to bed, not wanting to risk a premature labor. The following month, seven weeks before her due date, she developed toxemia, and was rushed to Baylor Hospital in Dallas.

Toxemia, or pre-eclampsia, is pregnancy-induced high blood pressure that occurs in about 5 to 10 percent of pregnancies. Laura fell into two risk-factor categories for the disease: having her first child, and being over thirty-five (if only slightly). Toxemia causes swelling and can lead to liver and kidney damage, fluid in the lungs, and, in the most severe cases, seizures and death.

Laura was monitored closely in the hospital as her toxemia grew more serious. She was forced to stay in bed for more than two months, but she kept up her spirits, according to her friend Pam Nelson. "She wasn't in a depression," said Pam. "She was in a very hopeful . . . determined, spirit [of] 'this is going to happen and it's going to be all right.'" Another of Laura's close friends, Regan Gammon, witnessed how difficult the ordeal was for George. "I think it was probably harder on George than it was on Laura," she said.[1]

By late November, Laura's toxemia had escalated and she was very ill. The doctor called George at work in Midland on November 24 and told him to get to Dallas the next day because "you are going to have your children tomorrow."

George asked, "Are you sure? It's five weeks early." The doctor said, "Well, unless you want your wife's kidneys to fail."[2]

The doctor scheduled a caesarean section. At about 10 A.M.

on November 25, 1981, their fraternal twins, Barbara and Jenna, were born. George and Laura were overjoyed.

Barbara arrived first, at five pounds four ounces, then Jenna, at four pounds twelve ounces. Laura's toxemia abated—giving birth is the only cure for the disease—and the babies and mother were fine.

George later recalled that Laura said, "These babies are going to be born healthy." He confessed that he was in awe over how she handled those agonizing weeks before their birth.

"She had that West Texas determination," he said on *The Oprah Show*. "I'm kind of tearing about it because it was such a powerful statement by a mother who said these children will come to be. It was such a resolute, powerful statement of motherhood. When the babies came and they were healthy and she was healthy, it was a fabulous moment."[3]

Laura's mother was impressed with George's dedication to his new family. "In the weeks that Laura was in the hospital, George went back and forth between Dallas and their home in Midland," Laura's mother recalled. "He had a room in a hotel across from Baylor Hospital but he'd fly back to Midland to carry on his work. He was also chairman of the Midland United Way that year, so he couldn't stay in Dallas all the time.

"He called me in tears the morning the girls were born and said, 'We have two beautiful babies!' And you know, nature is so wonderful. If there's trouble with the pregnancy, it will speed up the development of the babies. The hospital was prepared to put the twins in incubators but they just started breathing on their own. They were never in an incubator for a minute."[4]

George and Laura took their new daughters home and hired a part-time nurse to help for the first few months. When it was

George's turn to hold the twins as they cried, the only thing he could think to do was to sing Yale fight songs, such as "Bulldog, bulldog! Fight fight fight!"

"Babies don't come with sets of instructions," said Laura in a speech in August 2000. "Before George and I were married, we had a couple of theories on raising kids. Now we've got a couple of kids and no theories."[5]

Laura's days were filled with taking care of the twins, pushing their stroller up and down Golf Course Road, and enjoying daily visits from her father. "They were crazy about Harold," said Jenna Welch. "I didn't go by every day because I had other things to do and I didn't want to intrude on her life. But every day he ran by to see the girls after they were born."[6]

Their other grandparents, Vice President and Barbara Bush, now based in Washington, D.C., were able to fly to Midland six weeks after the girls were born. The birth of the babies had received national news coverage because of their famous grandfather, and George remarked that they "held their first press conference two hours after they were born."

Laura had survived a difficult pregnancy, and now, life was idyllic as she worked in her garden, raised her daughters, and spent time with her parents and lifelong friends. They often had dinner with Laura's parents, going back and forth between each other's homes.

The best times were the mornings, when they shared time together with their babies. "When they were infants," said Laura, "we would put them in bed with us in the mornings and George and I would each hold one of them. I love those memories."[7]

As an only child, Laura had learned how to enjoy her own

company and relish quiet hours by herself. Now, in her earliest years of motherhood, she cherished the peacefulness of her domestic life.

"When Barbara and Jenna were babies," she said, "I'd still have a few hours of light after they went to bed. One night I was in the garden, the babies were asleep, safe in their beds, and I remember thinking, 'This is the life.'"[8]

Family visits had long played a prominent role in Laura's life, and she cherished her closeness with her mother and father. "When Laura and George were first married," said Laura's mother, "they lived about eight blocks away from us and we'd see them nearly every day. Before they had the children they'd come over and have supper or we'd go to their place, and after dinner we'd play cards—hearts—at the kitchen table. Harold and George were partners and they always beat us unless we got awfully lucky.

"My husband was so delighted to have grandchildren, and I know Laura has told many people about his late morning visits. Poor Laura would get them down for their naps at about 11 A.M., just get them settled down and asleep, and Harold would come over and open the front door and call out, 'Are the girls awake?' And of course, they were then."[9]

From the first days of her marriage, Laura was very happy to be part of a large family for the first time in her life. "Laura just loved it when she married into a big family. For the first few Christmases she had more fun buying gifts for George's brother and sister. Then they all married and it got too big, so one year they said, 'Laura, let's not give gifts.' But she loved being there in Maine for Christmas with the whole big family. The Bushes are wonderful, easy people to know."[10]

❖ ❖ ❖

FOUR OF LAURA and George's best friends, Joe and Jan O'Neill and Don and Susie Evans, gathered with them for a mutual fortieth birthday bash in July 1986 in Colorado Springs. A friend, Penny Sawyer, and George's brother, Neil, joined the party as well. Everyone stayed at the Broadmoor Hotel, the opulent, 700-room lakeside resort built in 1918 at the foot of the Rocky Mountains.

The plan was to celebrate several of their birthdays over dinner on Saturday night and get up the next morning to visit the Air Force Academy Chapel, an architectural wonder and popular local attraction. The partying took its toll on George, who had a crushing hangover the next morning.

"I had a little too much to drink that night and woke up the next morning to go for a jog," he told Oprah. "I like to exercise a lot. And I made up my mind on that jog that I was going to give up drinking for the rest of my life. The best explanation is to say that alcohol was beginning to compete for my affections—compete for my affections with my wife and my family. It was beginning to crowd out my energy and I decided to quit, and it's one of the best decisions I ever made."[11]

Several times Laura told reporters, in jest, that George quit after that big night because he got the bar bill. However, another version began to circulate during the presidential campaign in 2000—that Laura had delivered an ultimatum to George, saying, "It's me or the Jim Beam." George was to have then made an "official" announcement to his friends at the hotel that he was quitting.

Laura refuted that version, saying that he didn't actually

talk about his decision until about three weeks later, at home with her.

"I'd been talking for a while about him quitting drinking," she told *Texas Monthly* writer Paul Burka. "I don't remember any announcement. I actually remember it more at home than at the Broadmoor."[12]

In response to one of the many journalists who have asked her about George's drinking, Laura has characterized it this way: "He was wild when he drank too much, I think."[13] She went on to say that he was disciplined in everything he did, except his drinking. When George finally decided to apply his strong sense of discipline to quitting, it worked. She elaborated on this when ABC's Cookie Roberts asked her how he managed to just stop one day, when so many people struggle with the problem.

"Because he has really incredible discipline," Laura answered. "George is very, very disciplined, and at that point in his life he was very disciplined about everything. He was already a runner. He'd been a runner for about fifteen years before that . . . and I think he just realized that alcohol was making—was competing for his affections, and was making him have . . . no energy, not the energy he wanted to have, and so he quit."[14]

In *A Charge to Keep*, George explained that he developed the will to quit over a year's time after a moving talk with the Reverend Billy Graham. In the summer of 1980, Reverend Graham had spent a weekend visiting the Bush family at Kennebunkport.

"One evening my dad asked Billy to answer questions from a big group of family," said George. "He sat by the fire and talked. And what he said sparked a change in my heart. . . . Over the course of that weekend, Reverend Graham planted a mustard seed in my soul, a seed that grew over the next year."[15] Laura and George had been active in the Methodist Church throughout their marriage, and after Dr. Graham's visit, George also joined a men's community Bible study group with Don Evans (whom he would appoint Commerce Secretary when he won the presidency) and other friends.

At the same church, Laura became a member of the Committee on Nominations and George served on the Administrative Board. They also participated in a Focus on the Family series about raising children.

Family life came first for Laura as a wife and mother in the 1980s. She drove in a carpool, worked on the PTA, and put in hours at her daughters' school library. Later, when the press asked her about her teacher/librarian/housewife background, she was proud to say that she felt satisfied "doing what really traditional women do."

In 1987, George, Laura, and their daughters moved to Washington, D.C., so that George could help his father with his presidential campaign. It was the first time Laura lived in the same city as her in-laws, and she began to form a close friendship with Barbara.

One day, while working on his father's ultimately successful campaign, George got a call from his former business partner back in Midland, Bill DeWitt. Bill had heard that the Texas Rangers baseball team was up for sale, and suggested that it would be a perfect business for George to get into. The current owner, seventy-eight-year-old Eddie Chiles, was an old friend of the Bush family who had once flown George's cancer-stricken sister Robin to the hospital in his private plane.

George immediately took to the idea and began to look for investors to come up with the $86-million selling price. He moved the family to Dallas and succeeded in putting together a partnership of several investors to buy the franchise, including Bill DeWitt and Mercer Reynolds who had worked with him in Midland.

As a managing partner, George handled all the public relations work and was the most visible member of the managing group. The owners worked with the franchise as a business property and did not get involved in running the team. "We would let the baseball people make the baseball decision," George said. "We didn't tell our managers whom to play at third base."

The biggest and most profitable deal George W. Bush helped launch as a managing partner was a new stadium. The Rangers, the American League team located in Arlington, 20 miles west of Dallas, were playing in a dilapidated ballpark that had been designed for the minor leagues.

The new owners' dream was to build a beautiful, state-of-the-art outdoor stadium designed in the spirit of old ballparks with an asymmetrical field length, fan seating located closer to the field, and other traditional details. They envisioned a baseball-only ballpark in a sports compound that featured a restaurant, office complex, museum, children's center, and other amenities that would improve the earning power of the stadium.

The deal came through with a voter-approved tax and bond program, and the Ballpark in Arlington opened in April 1994. George's behind-the-scenes work helped create what

Financial World magazine heralded as the most profitable facility in baseball.

Although Laura hadn't been a baseball fanatic the way George was while growing up, she and her parents had enjoyed the game. "We would watch Little League games," recalls her mother, "and we watched high school baseball. One year, when Laura was in high school, her team won their district and went on to play for the state championship. We took Laura and one of her friends to Austin for the games—and it rained. When our team finally got up for their first game, they lost. We had all hung around for just that one game—but it was still fun."

Laura went to fifty to sixty Rangers games a year with George for five years. "I always say," wrote George, "if you're going to a baseball game, you had better go with someone you like, because you have ample time to talk. I went with someone I loved. And talk we did: about baseball, about our girls, about life. . . . Our girls grew up at the ballpark."[16]

Laura grew to love the sport because it was a low-key, cozy way to spend the evenings with her family. "It was fun going to sixty-odd games a year," she said. "Baseball's so slow, you can daydream. It's a very relaxing evening."[17]

"Harold and I went with them to several games," said Laura's mother. "It was a wonderful life because we would sometimes go out to have dinner at the park's private club before going down to our seats right down in front."

One night, recalls Jenna Welch, she learned from Laura that it's a tradition to chew bubble gum at a baseball game. "The bat boys gave Laura and George bubble gum, and that night they were both intently watching the game and blew big bubbles at the same time. I leaned forward and told her that that didn't look very dignified, and she turned around and said, 'Mother, bubble gum is a tradition!'"

This was a turning point in George's life. For the first time, he had achieved business success and made a mark as his own man. When he sold the team in 1998, he received $15 million.

"Before the Rangers," said Roland Betts, one of his baseball franchise partners, "I told him he needed to do something to step out of his father's shadow. Baseball was it."

In Dallas, the Bushes lived on a tree-lined, affluent Northwood Road in a large house with a swimming pool. Their home was less than twenty blocks from Southern Methodist University, located directly south of them in University Park, where Laura had spent four years earning her undergraduate degree. Never had she dreamed that she would one day return to that posh corner of Dallas with a family of her own.

Every morning, George got up early, took a run, made coffee, and brought it to Laura in bed. In later years, he would follow the same routine at the Governor's Mansion and the White House. Their partnership brought out the best in them both, and Laura's role has been nothing less than "his safety net for life," according to one close adviser.

"Golly, she calmed him down," said her father-in-law, George H. W. Bush. Their friend Joe O'Neill, who has known George the longest and brought the couple together, has also witnessed how Laura mellowed George.

"Once you find the right person, that part of the equation is done and you can get on with the other things," he said. "There's no burning ambition there. She's not pushing George from the back, but she truly changed him."[18]

In April 2000, *Texas Monthly's* Paul Burka added, "She
will be hard-pressed to have as much influence over his life and
career as she has already had. Without her, he would not be
where he is."

Laura simply acknowledges, "He's so much more gregarious, talkative, and funny than I am. But we really complement
each other. . . . We find a lot of refuge in our relationship."[19]

George summed up the crucial balance that Laura brings to
his life in an interview during his presidential campaign. "[She
has] a reassuring calm. As a man who goes about a hundred
miles an hour, I find that attractive. . . . Politics doesn't totally
consume her, and as a result, it doesn't totally consume me."[20]

As co-owner of the Texas Rangers, George had lived a
boyhood dream, owning a piece of the great American pastime.
He and Laura had never been happier. Striking gold in baseball
had been the opportunity of a lifetime. But another opportunity
would soon appear on the horizon—one with irresistible allure,
and one that would forever change their lives.

CHAPTER 6

First Lady
of Texas

*"Few can dispute that Laura Bush
has been the best First Lady in years
and years, maybe ever."*
—TIME MAGAZINE, ON
LAURA BUSH'S YEARS AS
FIRST LADY OF TEXAS

WHEN, IN 1993, GEORGE W. BUSH first started talking to Laura about running for Governor of Texas, she was concerned about his motives. After sixteen years of marriage, she was fully entrenched in the Bush family and well aware of the effect its legacy had on its sons. The political pedigrees of his father and grandfather had established a towering standard of achievement, and Laura worried that her husband was trying to prove something for its own sake, rather than seeking out for what he truly wanted.

In recalling their private discussions about the governor's race in 1993, George said, "My wife was initially dubious; she wanted to make sure others weren't pushing me into the race and that campaigning for Governor was something I really wanted to do."

He assured her that he cared deeply about Texas and wanted to give back to make a difference. Buoyed by his success in the business world, he now had new confidence in himself and wanted to achieve his objectives in political office. His work with the Rangers had finally given him the financial security and personal accomplishment that his father and grandfather had built before they entered political life.

Laura was also very reticent about exposing her family to the attacks of a big campaign. She had witnessed her father-in-law's two presidential campaigns at close range and couldn't shake the hard, cold reality of character-bashing at the center of much political campaigning.

"Nineteen ninety-two was a miserable year for us," she said of George H. W.'s second presidential campaign, "because we saw a man we loved characterized in a way he wasn't." Laura didn't think she could bear watching her husband suffer the same treatment in a high-profile state campaign.

"I don't think anyone particularly likes to constantly hear their spouse criticized," said Laura's friend Regan Gammon, "or things said about them that are untrue."[1] They had already had a taste of the Yankee-bashing tactics of the opposition in the congressional campaign of 1977, and the race for governor would be even more high-profile because, in 1993, George was the son of a former president.

George determinedly entered the race and went on to beat the enormously popular incumbent, Ann Richards. But as Laura feared, the race was full of attacks on George's background, including Richards' famous barb that he "was born with a silver foot in his mouth."

Laura had supported her husband by giving speeches at Republican Women's Clubs across the state, but she didn't immerse herself in campaigning. "She wasn't really comfortable doing a lot of campaigning," wrote George in his autobiography, "which was fine with me."

When she did have to campaign, she spoke well and stressed her husband's education goals. Laura's philosophy, as described by her mother-in-law, is, "you can either like it or not, so you might as well like it." This is the kind of resolve she brought to all the challenges of entering public life as the First Lady of Texas.

Laura and George, who make up pet names for each other such as "Bushie," tease each other a lot, and during the gubernatorial campaign George made a joke about her profession. He said that as a librarian, her idea of a speech was saying "Shhhh!" to children. She called him on it, pointing out that it only perpetuated the stereotype of librarians as mean disciplinarians, and he stopped using the joke in speeches.

She still got back at him in one of her own. "To kid him, to get back at him, I said he was a gregarious businessman who thought that a bibliography was the biography—the story—of the person who wrote the Bible," she laughingly recalled.[2]

George didn't push Laura into making public appearances or devoting herself to programs or anything else that she didn't want to do as First Lady. "I wanted Laura to do only what she wanted to do, no more and no less," he said. "I didn't want my decision to lead a public life to dictate her choices."[3]

Laura decided to focus on new activities that would make the best use of her background and experience with books and reading, and she got started immediately—during the inauguration festivities. Her first act as First Lady of Texas was to arrange for seven Texas writers to give readings at the Capitol as part of the celebration. She realized that they may not have voted Republican, but politics were not part of her itinerary. Besides, the inauguration took place after the campaign, and being involved in the readings showed support for Texas culture, not for a candidate.

Novelist Sarah Bird introduced her reading by saying, "I just have to say how impressed I am y'all would invite a raging liberal like me . . . gives me a lot of hope for this administration."[4]

Laura was asked to give a speech at the reading, and she

was so nervous about it that she admits having had an anxiety dream the night before. These readings were a hint at the book festival she would launch later in George's first term—a cultural event that would become her biggest legacy.

When the Bushes moved into the Governor's Mansion in Austin on January 17, 1995, they became the thirty-eighth family to live there since the home was built in 1856. The builder, Abner Cook, had worked for two years on the two-story Greek Revival structure that faced the street with an imposing set of twenty-nine-foot Ionic columns. A deep porch stretched out from the red brick front, and the entrance was just a few steps away from the Colorado River, around which the city is built.

The Mansion is the oldest continuously occupied government residence west of the Mississippi and a National Historic Landmark. Thirteen years before the Bushes moved in, the house had undergone a major repair and refurbishing process and had been outfitted with a large collection of American antiques. Famous Texas heirlooms housed in the Mansion include Stephen F. Austin's writing desk, a snuff box owned by Sam Houston (governor of Texas, 1859–1861), and Governor Edmund Jackson Davis's Civil War–era sword (governor of Texas, 1870–1874).

The parade of First Ladies that has passed through the house includes Miriam Amanda Wallace Ferguson, whose husband, James E. Ferguson, was elected in 1914. Miriam made history when she was elected governor herself. Her husband was impeached and tried to get his name on the ballot again in 1924, but when the Supreme Court rejected his request, his wife ran for the office.

She promised voters that they would get "two governors for the price of one," and defeated the pro-Klan nominee in the Democratic runoff. She easily defeated the Republican candidate in the general election and became the first woman governor of Texas, and the second in the United States (after Wyoming's Nellie Ross).

Perhaps the most literary Texas First Lady was Frances Cox Henderson, whose husband, James Pinckney Henderson, was governor from 1846 to 1847—the first governor of the new state. The Governor's Mansion had not yet been built, so they lived on their plantation near St. Augustine during Henderson's term. Frances was born in Philadelphia but educated in France, after her parents discovered her exceptional abilities in math and languages. Frances spoke eighteen languages fluently and was a lifelong learner, taking up Russian when she was sixty. She published two books, *Priscilla Baker: Freed Woman* (1874), the story of a black woman based on Frances's experiences living on a plantation, and *Epitome of Modern European Literature* (1882), a translation of short stories.

During Laura Bush's second term as First Lady of Texas, Southern Methodist University awarded her a Distinguished Alumna award. She is also memorialized at the university with the Laura Bush Promenade, a tree-lined walkway outside the Fondren Library Center. George gave the university $250,000 to construct the walkway in his wife's honor, and it was completed in the spring of 1999. She learned about the Promenade the previous Christmas, when George presented her with a porcelain replica of the library and told her what was being built.

At the award ceremony in October 1999, Laura played

down her role as a "distinguished" graduate of the School of Humanities and Sciences. She told the audience that she proudly earned her degree from SMU but "may have married into the 'distinguished' part."[5]

Laura's passion for literature motivated the many programs she either launched or supported in her two terms as First Lady. One of her most far-reaching programs, the First Lady's Family Literature Initiative, created new Texas legislation on early childhood reading. She organized a conference and worked with both Republicans and Democrats to create a $215 million fund for new programs including "Ready to Read" and "Take Time for Kids."

"We simply knew it was Laura Bush's bill," said Texas Representative Paul Sadler, a Democrat. "She was very much at the forefront, and knew the subject very well." The Governor's Senior Education Adviser, Margaret LaMontage, recalled the effective way Laura worked with the legislators to team them up with literacy experts and build a realistic program. "[She] germinated the beginnings of this early childhood initiative by involving—you know, just like her husband does—the right people in the issue."[6]

In a press release on July 28, 1998, Laura reported on the goals and results to-date of her literary initiative as launched by House Bill 1640. Following is an excerpt:

> The governor and I want every Texas child to learn to read by the end of the third grade and continue reading at grade level or better throughout his or her school career.
> The battle, however, must be waged on two fronts, because there are Texas children *and* adults who cannot

read. A large number of Texas adults are at the bottom level of reading proficiency.

By promoting good reading instruction for young children, we can help break the cycle of illiteracy.

Just as children should be reading more, so should entire families. Clearly, adult literacy goes hand in hand with children's literacy. Literate adults can do a better job of meeting the daily needs of their families. And parents and other adults are instrumental in helping children develop an appreciation for reading.

As author James Baldwin said, "Children have never been good at listening to their elders, but they have never failed to imitate them."

The literacy initiative was codeveloped by Barbara Bush, who had launched a national program during her tenure as First Lady in the White House.

"My mother-in-law took an interest," said Laura in a speech in 1996, "and you know what happens when Barbara Bush gets involved in something. With support from the Barbara Bush Foundation for Family Literacy, we created . . . projects designed to create families of learners. Projects, which put a book in the center of the family circle."

In the same speech, she revealed two unique literacy programs she enacted in Texas: "Through a program called 'experience corps,' retired senior citizens put their wisdom and experience to work, helping low-income children learn to read. Boy Scouts and Girl Scouts took up the challenge, committing thousands of volunteer hours in one-on-one tutoring or group projects."

Laura's efforts on behalf of Texas children also included promoting a program for abused and neglected children called Greater Texas Community Partners. This organization, run by the state's Department of Child Protective Services, supports caseworkers who work with abused children and their families.

The agency sets up volunteer-run "Rainbow Rooms" where child-abuse caseworkers can get free clothes, diapers, formula, and other supplies for children. Rainbow Rooms are store-like settings run by volunteers and were originally conceived by a county program in Dallas that was launched in 1989. The state-wide program has spread to more than seventy cities.

Another Community Partners program that Laura advocated in speeches and appearances throughout the state is Adopt-A-Caseworker, in which child-abuse caseworkers are aligned with a business, church, or school to receive materials and support for their work. The adopting group gives the caseworker baby supplies or other tangible goods as well as the emotional support that is so needed in this type of work.

Laura served on several boards during her two terms as First Lady of Texas and continues her work with some of them. She is still on the Advisory Council of her alma mater, the University of Texas Graduate School of Library and Information Science, as well as Reading Is Fundamental Inc.

RIF is the nation's oldest children's literacy organization, run by a grassroots network of more than 300,000 volunteers who distribute new, free books to families, help prepare young children for reading, and motivate school-age children to read.

Women's health organizations in which Laura was involved included the breast-cancer awareness campaign of the Governors' Spouses Program. During the first year of her term, the Center for Disease Control launched a national campaign with the Governors' Spouses group to enhance public awareness of breast cancer and early detection. Laura hosted a women's forum in October 1994, National Breast Cancer Awareness Month, that gave Texas women an opportunity to voice their concerns about breast health and breast cancer, and learn what positive steps women can take to ensure good breast health.

She also actively supported the programs of the Susan G. Komen Breast Cancer Foundation, a national organization founded in 1980 by Nancy Brinker in memory of her sister, Susan Goodman Komen, who died from breast cancer.

Nancy is one of the nation's leaders in the fight against breast cancer, and her foundation has raised nearly $40 million for breast cancer research, screening, education, and treatment. One of the most visible fundraising activities of the foundation is the Race for the Cure, through which sponsored volunteer runners raise money for the Koman foundation's research grants and many education programs.

As an art lover, Laura promoted Texas artists—and raised her husband's level of appreciation for art. George encouraged Laura's enjoyment of baseball and she inspired in him a new taste for art, particularly paintings of Texas and the West. "He takes seriously what she takes seriously," said Bush friend and El Paso art gallery owner Adair Margo. "He has become very articulate and talks about art with great intelligence."[7]

Texas has a poor track record of government financial support for the arts. For several years it ranked last in arts spending among the fifty states and has thereby delegated most of the state's art funding to private and corporate sources. Laura Bush may have begun reversing this trend, however. In 2000, the Texas Commission on the Arts distributed $7.3 million, compared to $4.1 in 1996.

Laura's taste in art is both varied and spontaneous—she knows what she likes when she sees it, whether it's the work of a well-known American artist or an unknown local painter.

"Their taste is less formal and more contemporary," said Adair. "And they have a real taste for Latino and Mexican art. The Bushes are very rooted, and their history is rooted here."

During his acceptance speech for the Republican nomination in 2000, George quoted one of his favorite Texas artists, Tom Lea. "My friend, the artist Tom Lea of El Paso, Texas, captured the way I feel about our great land, a land I love. He said, 'Live on the east side of the mountain. It's the sunrise side. It is the side to see the day that is coming, not to see the day that has gone.'"

The Bushes boosted Lea's popularity when they began collecting his paintings—many of which depict the Old West—and displaying them at both the Governor's Mansion and the Capitol.

Laura also showcased Texas artists in her office at the Capitol, virtually turning it into another Austin gallery with rotating exhibits that highlighted several artists throughout the year. Each year she chose a Texas artist to create an illustration for the Governor and First Lady's Christmas cards.

In 2000, for example, she selected Linda Boudreaux Montgomery to illustrate the Governor's Mansion for the holiday cards. Montgomery had previously been invited to show her paintings in a solo exhibit at the Capitol.

Laura's interest in art extends to other mediums as well, such as sculpture, which she celebrated in a Capitol exhibition of the works of Austin sculptor Mary Paige Huey. Laura also worked with the Texas Capitol Historical Art Committee to collect art treasures from throughout the state and add them to the Capitol collection.

As a hard-working First Lady of Texas, Laura preferred to use her energy to create new legislation on behalf of children, rather than promote herself or assume the role of high-society hostess. Throughout George's two terms at the Governor's Mansion, there was not one black-tie event. Instead, the First Couple of Texas preferred casual entertaining, hosting barbecues that included barbecued ribs, hot dogs, and Laura's home-made chili.

During his re-election campaign in 1998, George often repeated, "There are many reasons I want people to re-elect me as Governor of Texas. The most important one may be to keep Laura Bush as our First Lady."

Later, when Laura made a speech at the Republican National Convention in 1996 in San Diego, the overwhelmingly warm response she received prompted George to say, "The same thing that happened to my old man has happened to me. Both our wives are far more popular than we are."[8]

"Now that they're in Washington," said Laura's mother, "I look back and think how easy it was in Austin. Things weren't so hectic—George just walked out the back and went to the Capitol, and then he'd come home for lunch. Laura and her friends would walk out the front gate and down the street to the river. Sometimes they'd walk all the way around Twin Lake, a four-mile walk."[9]

Laura Bush worked tirelessly for her causes—literacy, the public library system, women's health, and Texas art and writers. As a result, she was a very popular First Lady of Texas. "Her new role as First Lady [of the United States] might produce its share of anxiety dreams," wrote *Time* magazine, "but judging by her years as First Lady of Texas, she will prevail. . . ."[10]

CHAPTER 7

The Run
for President

*"George is a leader who brings
out the best in others, and he will inspire the
best in this country."*
—LAURA BUSH

B Y THE TIME GEORGE W. HAD DECIDED to run for President in 2000, Laura had made peace with her responsibilities as the wife of a very public figure. But with the new high-profile campaign for the presidency came a new level of concern about the darker side of that notoriety—the vicious personal attacks that often surface in a national campaign. The thought of her husband coming under the same fire as had his father in his two presidential campaigns disturbed Laura.

Later she confessed her original hesitation about George's run. "Many of you know that I was somewhat reluctant initially about this presidential campaign," she told reporters. "I was worried about its impact on our family. I knew it would be hard to see someone I loved criticized."[1] But she overcame those hesitations and set out on the campaign trail, delivering speeches in solo tours to thirty cities and accompanying George to thirty more.

During the Republican National Convention, at which Laura would make the biggest speech of her life to that day, 400 protestors gathered outside the Convention Center to draw attention to social issues such as flaws in the criminal justice system and the lack of public discussion on human rights abuses by the police and in the prison system. It was a peaceful demonstration, but arrests were made, and many people were angry over what they felt was an excessive reaction by the authorities.

Inside, events flowed smoothly, although everyone had
seen the protestors on their way in. It would not be the last time
Laura would be insulated from her husband's opponents—
during an appearance in Los Angeles soon after the inauguration she was swept away in a white SUV by Secret Service
agents, to avoid a small group of protestors riled about the con-
troversial election.

Being in public life has taken Laura far from her safe,
small-town roots, but the work she is accomplishing undoubt-
edly makes it worthwhile.

In her speech during the second session of the convention,
Laura Bush shared several facts about her West Texas childhood, including who she was, where she was going, and why
she believed in George W. Bush. Dressed in a cheerful lime-
green suit, she took her place center stage where cameras
zoomed in on her laughing green eyes and microphones picked
up her soft Texan drawl. Providing an appropriate backdrop
behind her were rows of students sitting at desks, further estab-
lishing the teacher and librarian career roles that had been
Laura's life before she married George.

When the crowd's welcome ovation wore on too long,
Laura slipped into her firm-but-friendly teacher mode by
putting up her hands and saying, "All right now, quiet down."
Everyone quickly complied—like a massive grammar school
assembly hushed by the principal. She then proceeded to charm
her audience with her warmth, humor, and obvious devotion to
her husband and family, as well as her personal goals—which
would one day impact every student in America.

Confessing to being "a little overwhelmed," she then
proceeded to charm her audience by declaring that "You

know I am completely objective when I say . . . you have made a great choice."

At that time, they had been married for twenty-three years. Their lives had undergone tremendous changes during that period: George had been elected governor of Texas, the family had moved to Austin with their lively thirteen-year-old twin daughters, and the couple was now helping Barbara and Jenna pack for college.

"They say parents often have to get out of the house when their kids go off to college because it seems so lonely. Everyone deals with it in different ways. But I told George I thought running for president was a little extreme," she quipped.

Then, switching gears, she made a reference to her personal passion—a subject America would hear a lot more about in years to come. "I have never had this many people watch me give a speech before, but I feel very at home here in this classroom setting," she confided. "Education is the living room of my life."

Wryly, she added, to the delight of her audience, "George's opponent has been visiting schools lately and sometimes when he does, he spends the night before at the home of a teacher. . . . well, George spends *every* night with a teacher."

Teaching was more than a profession to Laura Bush. It was a moral and personal commitment to bettering America's youth. She confided her earliest aspirations to her audience.

"Growing up, I practiced teaching on my dolls. I would line them up in rows for the day's lessons. Years later, our daughters did the same thing. We used to joke that the Bush family had the best-educated dolls in America."

Laura then offered her listeners a rare glimpse into the Bush's family life. "George and I always read to our girls— Dr. Seuss's *Hop on Pop* was one of his favorites. George would like on the floor and the girls would literally hop on Pop," turning storytime into a contact sport.

Although Texas had been criticized for its poor showing in education, Laura staunchly refuted this in her remarks, crediting her husband with impressive improvements in her home state's literacy. "A highly respected, nonpartisan RAND study released just last week found our education reforms in Texas have resulted in some of the highest achievement gains in the country, among students from all racial, socioeconomic, and family backgrounds," she reported proudly.

Laura Bush knew how difficult it is for a teacher to do her job when a child can't read. In fact, when she had taught school in Austin and Houston, some of the second, third, and fourth grade students were illiterate. "I tried to make it fun by making the characters in children's books members of our class," she said. "We saved a web in the corner for Charlotte."

She then made a personal pledge to America's parents— one that she and George shared. "As First Lady, I will make early childhood development one of my priorities, and George will strengthen Head Start to make sure it's an early reading and early learning program."

A passion for children was not the only shared commitment. Both George and Laura brought with them a

strong sense of community and family values. Having
hailed from Midland, a "small town in a vast desert," as
Laura described it, the couple knew that it was important for
Americans to be able to depend on each other. For Laura,
Midland's value reserves were "as deep and longer-lasting
than any of its oil wells."

It was from the wellspring of Midland's values, she
declared, that the future president developed his strength and
the constancy of his convictions. "His core principles will
not change with the winds of polls or politics or fame or for-
tune or misfortune," she promised. "I know because I've
known him through big legislative successes and a few
defeats. I've sat by his side during some winning and many
losing baseball seasons. But George never loses sight of
home plate."

Laura then recalled looking through some old scrap-
books, struck by how little her husband, now vying for the
presidency, had changed since his run years earlier for Congress in West Texas. "[T]he things he said then are the same
things he believes now . . . that government should be limited . . . that local people make the best decisions for their
schools and communities . . . that all laws and policies
should support strong families . . . that individuals are
responsible for their actions."

She also confided that her husband was basically an opti-
mist, and that he conveyed this belief to those with whom he
worked. But most of all, Laura confided to her audience, her
husband was a man of purpose. "To quote the hymn that
inspired his book, he believes we all have "a charge to
keep"—a responsibility to use our different gifts to serve a

cause greater than self."

Finally, Laura closed her speech by describing a special moment she had during a recent visit to Crawford, where she and George had attended a high school graduation ceremony. "As I watched George visit with the graduates and their families, I thought . . . This is America. Down-to-earth people who work hard, who care for our neighbors, who want a better life for our children. And the people of America deserve a leader who lifts our sights, who inspires us to dream bigger and do more."

Cheers went up as Laura shook hands with those on the platform. George looked at his wife with the same admiring gaze he had worn as she walked down the aisle of the chapel in Midland's First United Methodist Church on their wedding day.

Over the years Laura brought up the subject of George's broken promise as a joke among family and friends about the political life she inherited. "I'd always say, 'So much for political promises,'" she told one reporter. But the promise she made in her wedding vows, to be his lifelong companion, carried over into their political life for better or for worse.

For George, it was clearly for the better, as he was in vital need of women's votes in Campaign 2000. Polls revealed that married women with children moved to the Republican side during the campaign, and political analysts credit Laura for much of this significant change.

Laura's effectiveness in softening the impression of the Republican Party—and of her husband—was a major "plus" during the campaign. Conservatives who had been put off by

Hillary Clinton's forcefulness and direct action in President Clinton's administration were relieved to meet Laura Bush, a woman with a comforting background of a teacher and librarian, and, most importantly, one without any political ambitions or agendas.

Laura Bush's participation in the presidential campaign was also vital to balance the rambunctious, frenetic, and sometimes crass impression given by her husband. For instance, after the September 11 attack by terrorists, many were chagrined when President Bush vowed to take America on a "crusade" against evil, not realizing that talk of a "crusade" would antagonize many of the same Moslems worldwide that the administration was trying to win over.

Laura's non-threatening career background and strong speaking skills were highly effective in winning more voters, as revealed in polls taken during the convention. In one poll, Voter.com's Battleground 2000, Bush's standing catapulted from a two-point deficit among women voters to a six-point lead over Gore three days into the convention. Republican pollster Ed Goeas stated that the strongest new wave of support identified by the polls was coming from "married, employed, white women with children."[2]

Laura's speeches during the presidential campaign were laced with indirect references to President Clinton in an attempt to contrast his values with those of her husband. With phrases that describe the President as "more than a man" and "the most visible symbol of our country . . . and its values," she promised the American public in her convention speech that George would bring new integrity to the office.

These subtle targets of comparison were highly successful

components of the Bush campaign.

Promoting family values was another high priority on Laura's itinerary when she joined George's presidential campaign trail in 1999. In her first appearance that summer, in Ames, Iowa, her speech contained more direct criticism of Clinton's scandal-ridden character than the convention address she would give later.

In Iowa and throughout the campaign, she gave speeches that focused on George Bush as the type of decent human being whom Americans needed to fill the highest office in the land. "Americans want somebody who they do trust, someone who they feel like won't embarrass them but instead will make them proud," she told the Iowa crowd. She revealed that she felt blessed to be married to "a man of strong conviction and strong faith who keeps his word and loves his family." Unlike her very first speech in Muleshoe, Laura's words were now very carefully chosen. She also had the benefit of twenty-three years of experience as a member of the Bush family behind her. "Governor Bush has represented Texas with dignity and honor," she said. "I'd love to see him do the same thing for our nation in its highest office."

That initial appearance, one month before Iowa's Republican straw poll election, set the tone for Laura's role in the presidential campaign. Not only would she spell out the contrasts between the two candidates; she would also embody the contrast between herself and Hillary Clinton. Her speeches reflected the calm firmness of a grade-school teacher whom most Americans would easily relate to and respect. Laura's stance as a woman who valued tradition, with a background in teaching—the most traditional career for a woman—struck a positive chord with conservatives from day one.

During Hillary Clinton's tenure in the White House, opinions about the role of the First Lady had become polarized, with one side expressing pride and inspiration over the fact that a woman had finally carved out a clear-cut, working role alongside her president husband that far exceeded the usual position of White House hostess or private sounding board; and the other side expressing fierce opposition to the idea of the President's wife overstepping the bounds of the roles of social hostess or her husband's private confidante.

George was clear about his position on the issue. During his run for governor, he described Laura as the "perfect" model of a governor's wife, someone who is not "trying to butt in and always, you know, compete. There's nothing worse in the political arena than spouses competing for public accolades or the limelight."[3] To the Bush family and the Republican Party, Laura Bush was the living, breathing incarnation of the traditional values they found so sorely lacking in the Clinton White House.

To underscore George's words, Laura took every opportunity to make it clear that she was not his adviser. "I don't give him a lot of advice," she told Barbara Walters during an ABC television interview. "I really don't think he wants a lot of advice from me." When George protested, saying that that was not true, she countered from another perspective, saying, "Well, I don't want a lot of advice from him."

In her convention speech, Laura wryly joked about the timing of George's decision to run for president, dubbing it a symptom of the "empty nest syndrome." But her husband knew that 1999 was his time. George had been dreaming of the presidency since he first ran for the congressional seat from West Texas in 1977. He came from a strong political background that included influential presidential advisers, a grandfather who served as a U.S. senator, and a father who had actually served as President of the United States. George felt he was ready to take on the challenges—and satisfactions—of the U.S. Presidency. He had no idea of the magnitude of responsibilities that awaited him—or the testing that lay ahead for his loved ones, and his country.

By the time she stepped up to the podium at the convention that summer night in Philadelphia, Laura Bush had not only forgiven George his broken promise and overcome her initial loathing of the spotlight—she had transformed herself into a vital, stabilizing force in the Bush political dynasty.

Laura had become a loyal member of the Bush family, but she retained her homey nature and her well-developed sense of self. "You could call one side, Laura and the other side, Bush," wrote Texas journalist Paul Burka, who has written about and attended social gatherings with the family. "Laura remains a woman who is down to earth, without affectation or pretension. . . . But the other side of her is that she is totally a Bush. Being a member of the clan has also been a central part of the education of Laura Bush."[4]

Laura Welch Bush is intelligent, well-read, organized, and unflappable; all the right tools for meeting important guests at the White House with aplomb. She has developed political savvy as the wife of a two-term governor and daughter-in-law of a president. And her career background, which can easily sound like a throwback to the 1950s, has its unconventional side.

"When I describe myself as traditional," she said, "I mean in the sense that I had jobs that were traditionally women's jobs. But I never felt I was so traditional. . . . For instance, teaching

*Baby Laura on the front
steps of her home at
704 North Loraine in
Midland, Texas, 1947.*

*Little Laura at her home at
408 West Estes, Midland.*

*Laura Welch,
two-year-old charmer.*

*Jenna and ten-year-old Laura Welch pose alongside
their mailbox in Midland in 1956.*

*Seventeen-year-old Laura
opening gifts, Christmas, 1963.*

*Laura with her parents,
Jenna and Harold Welch, 1963.*

Midland debutants, 1965 (left to right):
Gwyne Smith, Lucy McFarland,
Sally Brady, Laura Welch,
Jan Donnelly, Karen Huffman.

The happy graduate at her
SMU graduation, 1968.

Eighteen-year-old Laura Welch
with her dog, Rusty.

Laura during a trip to Exeter,
England, age twenty-four.

The Bushes, proudly holding twins Jenna (L) and Barbara (R).

A flyer for George Bush's first congressional campaign in 1978.

Laura and George W. Bush with Laura's mother, Jenna Welch, in the Governor's mansion in Austin, Texas, Christmas, 1997.

U.S. President George W. Bush, First Lady Laura Bush, and their twin daughters Barbara, far left, and Jenna greet supporters January 20, 2001 at the Florida Presidential Inaugural Ball at the National Building Museum.

Newly inaugurated President George W. Bush and First Lady Laura Bush dance at an Inaugural Ball.

From left to right, Hillary Rodham Clinton, President Bill Clinton, Laura Bush, and President-Elect George W. Bush before the presidential inauguration ceremony January 20, 2001 in Washington, DC.

First Lady Laura Bush reads to students at Morningside Elementary School, March 22, 2001, in San Fernando, CA.

An exuberant foursome: First Lady Laura Bush, U.S. President George W. Bush, Lynn Cheney, and Vice President Dick Cheney during a Republican National Committee Fundraiser Gala, May 22, 2001 in Washington DC.

(L to R) At the National Cathedral in Washington, DC., George W. Bush, Laura Bush, George and Barbara Bush, and Bill and Hillary Clinton mourn those lost on September 11.

First Lady Laura Bush speaks from the heart with Oprah Winfrey on the Oprah Winfrey Show, *taped September 18, 2001 in Chicago, IL.*

Laura speaks to the press after visiting with victims of the Pentagon terrorist airplane attack September 12, 2001 at Walter Reed Army Medical Center in Washington, DC.

In Pennsylvania, the First Lady addresses the media on September 17, 2001, following a memorial service for the families of the victims of Flight 93. Beside her are Pennsylvania Governor Tom Ridge and his wife, Michele.

in minority schools . . . not marrying until my thirties. I felt I was in many ways very contemporary."[5]

Laura's friends know a different woman from the one who appears serenely by her husband's side. "Mrs. Bush is a very pleasant person to be around," wrote Burka. "But I have some idea of what she is like around her friends, and we, that is, the media, never see that person. . . . We don't see her humor or her depth. She has always been intensely private, and . . . very much in control of herself."

Burka admitted that Laura's genuine niceness makes her good company, but not necessarily a hot scoop. "I have never heard anybody say a negative word about her," he said. "Sure makes life hard for the media—just kidding."[6]

CHAPTER 8
America's First Reader

"There's no magic like the magic of the written word."

—LAURA BUSH

SINCE THE TIME LAURA WAS BORN, books were a vital part of her life. Her mother, Jenna, had always loved to read, and when Laura came along, she quickly passed on her love of storytelling to her only child. "I read to her from the time she was a baby."[1] Those hours together, when her mother shared an amazing world of stories with her, would linger in her memory as a very special time.

Throughout her life, in both private and public sectors, Laura Bush has tried to bring her love of books to others. Literacy has become one of the passions she has brought to public office as First Lady of both Texas and the United States. If she has her way, it will become the cause with which she will make an indelible imprint upon the consciousness of this country.

From the time she was in grade school, Laura identified favorites to which she would refer others; among these were *The Secret Garden* by Frances Hodgson Burnett; *Little House on the Prairie, On the Banks of Plum Creek*, and other books in the Little House series by Laura Ingalls Wilder; and the Bobbsey Twins books created by Edward Stratemeyer.

"My mother read to me," said Laura, "and I think most people who love to read, or writers, had parents who loved to read. I remember my mother calling to say, 'Come set the table,' or come do something, and I couldn't put my book down; I had to keep reading."[2]

Often, when Laura had a friend over for the night, they

would bring snacks into Laura's room and read dramatic passages from their favorite books aloud to each other. "If I were asked what soggy crackers reminded me of, I'd say Louisa May Alcott's *Little Women*," said Laura's friend Georgia Temple. "I still see us propped up in a big double bed, eating crackers, while we read and reread Beth's death."

As Beth had hoped, the 'tide went out easily,' and in the dark hour before dawn, on the bosom where she had drawn her first breath, she quietly drew her last, with no farewell but one loving look, one little sigh.

Laura had more than one reason to admire Alcott. Not only did she write classics that are still enjoyed more than 130 years later, but she, too, made her living for a time as a schoolteacher.

Reading in bed was to become one of Laura's lifetime habits. "I've always read in bed," she told Susan Stamberg on National Public Radio in the summer of 2001. "I would go stretch out on my bed and read, whatever time of the day it was. And that's still where I read now. I also can remember, and not that long ago, reading in bed at night and glancing at the clock and finding out it's two in the morning and you've read too late."[3]

In an interview for *Time* magazine in June 2001, First Lady Laura Bush discussed more of her reading habits and her favorite titles. "I read every day, and I always read every night in bed—for thirty or forty minutes at the least." She admitted that sometimes the president has to ask her to turn out the light, or she has to ask him. "It depends on who's sleepiest," she said.

The book she was reading at the time of the interview was

Pearl S. Buck: A Cultural Biography by Peter J. Conn. "Pearl Buck was a very interesting writer," Laura told *Time* writer Lissa August. "I read *The Good Earth*, like everybody else did probably in high school, but there are a lot of things about her that I didn't know."

Laura reads mainly fiction and biography, while George prefers history and political biography. She mentioned that the president immediately started reading *In the Heart of the Sea: The Tragedy of the Whaleship Essex* by Nathaniel Philbrick, the National Book Award winner, after the author made a visit to the White House.[4]

Even though their main reading preferences may differ, Laura and George do share one passion—a love of mysteries. They sometimes come upon one that they feel compelled to pass along and share. Laura stated that she has read "millions of mysteries. . . . I love all of the famous British mystery writers, like Dorothy Sayers. And then I love a lot of American ones, like Mary Willis Walker, who happens to live in Austin."[5]

Laura reads *about* books, too, poring over the reviews and bestseller lists of the *New York Times Book Review* and other weeklies. She admits that, before buying a novel or other new title, "I nearly always have read book reviews" about the book first.

"I have a number of friends and relatives that I share books with, like my mother-in-law and Lynne Cheney." One of the books Laura and the vice-president's wife enjoyed sharing was *The Girl with the Pearl Earring* by Tracy Chevalier. "That's historical fiction about the artist Vermeer . . . and I did like it a lot," said Laura. "Then I just saw the Vermeer show at the Metropolitan. It was fabulous."[6]

In a July 2000 interview, the *New York Times* asked Laura to name her favorite book. She responded with *The Brothers Karamazov* by Feodor Dostoyevsky, and revealed that her favorite part of the book was the Grand Inquisitor section.[7]

What does this tell us about Laura Bush? Interestingly, the *Legend of the Grand Inquisitor*, a story made up by Ivan and told to his brother Alyosha, is considered the high point of Dostoyevsky's work. It addresses a fundamental Christian struggle, the choice between simply following the rules and regulations of organized religion (which substitutes its authority for a personal relationship with God) or developing the strength to follow the true path of Christ, a path of absolute freedom. The person who chooses freedom cannot fall back on the security of the church but must "decide for himself what is good and what is evil."

The story is also an allegory about socialism, a political system that provides the material necessities of life but does not address the spiritual.

The *Legend* has been a source of inspiration for Christians since Dostoyevsky published *The Brothers Karamazov* in 1879. That Laura Bush considers it her favorite work indicates her enjoyment of the mental gymnastics that Dostoyevsky demands of his readers. He brings up complex ideas and does not offer easy answers, but forces readers to interpret and understand for themselves.

Continuing the discussion of her favorite reading, Laura told *Time* magazine that she and George read four newspapers every morning: *The New York Times, Washington Post, Washington Times*, and *USA Today*. She also keeps up with news back home by taking a look at the *Dallas Morning News*.

In June 2001, the *Atlanta Constitution* asked the First Lady for a list of her favorite and recommended books that make great reading for the entire family. She responded with the following, which was published in the paper on June 4:

1. *The Little House* series by Laura Ingalls Wilder
2. *The Hank the Cowdog* series by John Erickson
3. *Goodnight Moon* by Margaret Wise Brown
4. *Officer Buckle and Gloria* by Peggy Rathmann
5. *If You Give a Pig a Pancake* by Laura Joffe Numeroff
6. *Old Yeller* by Fred Gipson
7. *Caddie Woodlawn* by Carol Ryrie Brink[8]

Laura's grade school years encompassed the Golden Age of Television in the 1950s, with kids' shows like *The Mickey Mouse Club*, *Superman*, and *Howdy Doody*; comedies such as *I Love Lucy* and *The Honeymooners*; family shows including *Ozzie and Harriet* and *Father Knows Best*; and the live comedy variety shows such as *Ted Mack's Original Amateur Hour*, *The Colgate Comedy Hour*, which often featured Dean Martin and Jerry Lewis, Art Linkletter's *People Are Funny*, *The Red Skelton Show*, and *Your Show of Shows* with Sid Caesar and Imogene Coco.

Much as she enjoyed TV in the 1950s, television could never match reading as Laura's favorite entertainment. Even today she reads much more than she watches television—except, perhaps, during baseball season. "We watch games on television a lot, usually the Texas Rangers. . . . I've watched *The Antiques Roadshow* a few times, but I'm not a regular watcher. I love *Mystery* on PBS, but I haven't watched it in a long time."[9]

In her second year as First Lady of Texas, Laura found a way to put her love of books to work for the state of Texas, specifically its public library system. In 1996, she launched the Texas Book Festival, an event that has become one of the country's premier literary events and has raised $1 million for the Texas libraries.

The idea of a festival honoring Texas authors struck deep chords in the First Lady both as a book lover and as a native Texan. It was an idea whose time had come, a perfect reflection of the cultural history she loved. "I think a part of our culture is that Texans love storytelling," she said. "We love to tell stories. We love to hear stories."[10]

Texas's literary tradition goes back to the 1800s with biographies and adventure stories such as *Colonel Crockett's Exploits and Adventures in Texas, by Himself* (1837)—actually written by Richard Penn Smith, it is a reasonably factual biography that brought the tale of Davy Crockett's heroic death at the Alamo to an American public that was hungry for the story.

One of the most widely read writers of the mid-1800s, Mayne Reid, wrote lively novels such as *The Rifle Rangers* (1850) and *The Scalp Hunters* (1851) based on his adventures in Texas and the American Southwest, and his experiences as a commissioned officer in the Mexican War. Edgar Allan Poe, who befriended Reid, described him as "a colossal but most picturesque liar. He fibs on a surprising scale but with the finish of an artist, and that is why I listen to him attentively."

John C. Duval, the first Texas man of letters, fought in the Mexican War and Civil War and served with the Texas Rangers. His *Early Times in Texas* (1892) is considered the most skillfully written and compelling of the personal adventure books of the era. Duval's other works include *The Adventures of Bigfoot Wallace, the Texas Ranger and Hunter* (1870), another classic of Texas literature.

O. Henry based some of his famous short stories, such as *A Departmental Case*, on his observations of Texas cowboys, outlaws, Texas Rangers, and sheriffs, made during his stay in the state. Another fiction writer, Texas native Dorothy Scarborough, made her mark with a novel set in West Texas. *The Wind* (1925) swept readers away with its realistic portrayal of ranchers' survival during the drought of 1885.

J. Frank Dobie, a major figure in 20th-century Texas literature, published his debut novel, *Vaquero of the Brush Country*, in 1929 and followed it with *Coronado's Children* (1931), which won the Literary Guild Award. Born on a ranch in Live Oak County, Texas, Dobie was introduced to books at an early age. He and his five brothers and sisters were read to by both parents—their father read from the Bible and their mother read aloud great books such as *Ivanhoe* and *Swiss Family Robinson*.

The First Lady can point to J. Frank Dobie, one of Texas' most prolific and beloved writers, as a perfect example of the enormous benefits of reading to children. Four days before Dobie's death, President Lyndon B. Johnson awarded him the Medal of Freedom, the United States' highest civil award.

Walter Prescott Webb, a prominent American historian and longtime professor of history at the University of Texas, has been called "his generation's foremost philosopher of the frontier, and the leading historian of the American West."[11] His twenty books include *The Great Plains* (1931), *The Texas Rangers, A Century of Frontier Defense* (1935), *Divided We Stand* (1937), and *The Great Frontier* (1952).

Another major voice from Webb's time is Katherine Anne Porter, a master of the short story whose first collections included *Flowering Judas* (1930) and *Pale Horse, Pale Rider* (1939). She released her first novel, *Ship of Fools*, in 1962. First Lady Laura Bush told an interviewer in July 2001 that she made a habit of rereading her all-time favorite books, and that she was currently rereading Porter's *Ship of Fools*.

J. Frank Dobie and Walter Prescott Webb teamed up with another friend and writer, Roy Bedicheck, to form the Texas Institute of Letters in 1936. This organization, self-described as one "whose purpose is to stimulate interest in Texas letters and to recognize distinctive literary achievement," continues to distribute thousands of dollars in literary awards to writers throughout the United States for fiction, nonfiction, poetry, short story, journalism, and children's books. The Texas Institute of Letters carries the legacy of the state's great literary triumvirate— Dobie, Webb and Bedicheck—and is an icon of Texas culture.

Contemporary luminaries of Texas writing include John Graves, author of *Goodbye to a River* (1960), *Hard Scrabble: Observations on a Patch of Land* (1974), and *From a Limestone Ledge: Some Essays and Other Ruminations about Country Life in Texas* (1980). Graves is sometimes called the "Texas Thoreau" and his most famous book, *Goodbye to a River*, was described by one journalist as "basically the Bible of our state."[12]

Horton Foote, a native of Wharton, Texas, received Oscars for his original Hollywood screenplay *Tender Mercies* (1983) and his screenplay adaptation of Harper Lee's *To Kill a Mockingbird* (1962). Author of books, plays, and film, Foote has won many other awards including a Pulitzer in drama.

Larry McMurtry won the Pulitzer Prize in 1986 for his historical novel *Lonesome Dove,* which was followed by *Streets of Laredo* and *Comanche Moon.* His novels of modern life include *The Last Picture Show* and *Terms of Endearment.*

Cormac McCarthy, who relocated to El Paso in 1976 and has lived there ever since, achieved royal status on the literary scene in 1992 with *All the Pretty Horses,* which won the National Book Award. The first in a trilogy, *Horses* was followed by *The Crossing* and *Cities of the Plain.*

Elmer Kelton, whose name is synonymous with the Western novel, has written thirty-seven books and received the Lone Star Award for Lifetime Achievement from the Larry McMurtry Center for Arts and Humanities in 1998.

This brief and far-from-complete sketch of important Texas writers hints at the motivation behind Laura Bush's passion to celebrate her home state's literary treasures. Great writers are one of Texas's great natural resources.

In late 1995, Laura used her resources as Texas's First Lady to bring together a task force that would turn her dream into reality. She played a hands-on role as Honorary Chairman of the Texas Book Festival, and continues to do so—even after moving to the White House.

The organizers, including festival chairman Mary Margaret Farabee, were concerned about the continuity of the event when George W. announced he was going to run for the presidency. They feared that Laura would be completely immersed in the campaign and would not have time to keep working on the festival.

They had no reason to worry; the festival is enormously important to Laura and she made time for it. Ms. Farabee recalled thinking to herself at the start of the presidential campaign, "Oh my gosh, we're not ever going to see her again. But she is remarkably accessible. It's something she believes in."[13]

The first Texas Book Festival was held in November 1996, and by the end of the festival in 2000 the event had raised more than $1 million, all of which was distributed to 394 Texas public libraries. Each year saw bigger crowds, and by the fourth year the event drew 25,000 to the Capitol in Austin. The festival succeeds in bringing together the most prominent writers in the country, including but not limited to Texas authors.

In the five festivals held from 1996 to 2000, more than 600 authors have given readings or participated in panel discussions, including Frank McCourt, Carlos Fuentes, John Graves, Larry McMurtry, David Halberstam, Stephen Harrigan, Sandra Cisneros, Chitra Banerjee Divakaruni, Mary Karr, Larry L. King, Jim Lehrer, Naomi Shihab Nye, Benjamin Alire Saenz, Mary Willis Walker, Rudolfo Anaya, Rick Bass, T. Coraghessan Boyle, Sandra Brown, Octavia Butler, Ana Castillo, Mary Higgins Clark, Stanley Crouch, Linda Ellerbee, Molly Ivins, David Lindsey, Michael Nesmith, Joan Lowery Nixon, Edward James Olmos, Louis Sachar, Jane Smiley, Whitley Strieber, and Scott Turow.

Each festival opens with the black-tie First Edition Literary Gala—a Texas-style, tuxedo-and-cowboy-boots wing-ding—held in the Austin Marriott next to the Capitol. For the $350 ticket price, guests are treated to cocktails and a multi-course dinner during which readings are given by famous writers.

At the 2000 gala, for example, historian Stephen Ambrose read from his new bestseller, *Nothing Like It in the World: The Men Who Built the Transcontinental Railroad*; J. California

Cooper, a native Texan, read from her new short story collection, *The Future Has a Past;* Stephen Harrigan discussed his new book, *The Gates of the Alamo*; and Liz Smith, the famous columnist, read from her new memoir, *Natural Blonde*.

The previous year, the 1999 gala included out-of-state authors for the first time. Speaking at the sold-out gala were Pulitzer Prize-winning authors David Halberstam (born in New York), author of *The Powers That Be*, and Frank McCourt (native of Ireland and longtime New Yorker), author of *Angela's Ashes*.

For the 2001 gala, authors invited to appear were Sara Bird, an award-winning Texas author whose novel, *Virgin of the Rodeo*, is being produced for a film by Warner Bros.; David McCullough, the Pulitzer Prize–winning author of *Truman*; and Ruth Reichl, *New York Times* food editor and author of *Tender at the Bone*.

Through the course of the evening, gala guests bid on silent auction items that included rare and collectible literary materials. In 1999, the silent auction alone raised $30,000 for the Texas Public Library System. After the gala, guests are invited to kick back at Austin's famous restaurant, Scholz Garten, for another party.

Money is also raised at the festival through the Bon Appetit Y'All Food Tasting and Cookbook Event and the Authors' Party. These two events, in addition to the gala, make up the three ticketed aspects of the festival. Proceeds from the ticketed events, book sales, and merchandise make up the funding that is given to the library system. The Texas Book Fair is the only festival in the country that functions as both a literary event and a fundraiser.

The bulk of the festival is situated in seven or eight large, circus-like tents placed on the Capitol grounds, and most of the activities are free. There is a tent for book signings with featured authors; an entertainment tent with live performances by Texas singer-songwriters and other performers; a tent filled with nearly 100 vendors including booksellers, small presses, independent and major publishers, writers' organizations, and many others; a children's tent featuring storytellers, book-related craft activities, and live entertainment; and a poetry tent.

The readings and panel discussions take place in the Capitol building itself, offering many attendees a chance to visit the Senate and House Chambers for the first time. This, perhaps more than the celebrity authors and autograph sessions and live music, makes the festival a very special experience for Texans.

"What really makes the whole festival—the gala and all the opening ceremonies included—is the fact that it's in our state Capitol," said Dr. William Tydeman, Associate Dean and Director of the Southwest Collection of the Special Collections Library at Texas Tech in Lubbock. "An awful lot of people who are book lovers around the state may not have been inside the Capitol before, and it's an extraordinary building. To wander around the Capitol and listen to authors and to interesting panel discussions in the chambers adds an enormous dynamic to the visit. The festival couldn't have a better setting. It speaks to the vision that First Lady Laura Bush had; of all the places she could have chosen, to create the festival at the Capitol was inspired."[14]

Dr. Tydeman attends the festival as a representative of the Special Collections Library as well as the publishing arm of the Book Club of Texas. The club, which is administered at the university, publishes fine-quality reprints of rare and classic Texas literature. Book Club of Texas Publications produces two titles per year, which are eagerly awaited by the bibliophiles, collectors, and all-around book lovers who make up the Book Club of Texas.

The Special Collections Library at Texas Tech houses the personal papers of several famous authors, and by exhibiting at the Texas Book Festival they introduce the public to the vast stores of Texas literary history contained in the library. "We have the best collection in the country of what we call literary natural-ists, writers often referred to as nature writers, although the authors themselves usually object to that categorization. These writers include Barry Lopez, Rick Bass, Bill McKibben, and Doug Peacock. We are also well-known to Texas scholars for our ranching collections, which contain the records of ranches from their first days to the modern era of corporate ranching."

Tydeman recalled a memorable event at the 2000 fes-tival—a personal appearance by John Graves, one of Texas's most famous and reclusive writers. "Getting John Graves there was quite a thrill because John is not a public speaker," he said. "He eschews the typical author circuit, but the festival orga-nizers and Rick Bass were able to convince him to do an inter-view. It was a fantastic opportunity to honor John Graves for his wonderful work. *Goodbye to a River* is a major work of Amer-ican writing, and that it happens to be from Texas is an addi-tional bonus. Just to see John Graves and have him honored was a real highlight for a lot of Texans."

Eighty-year-old John Graves was awarded the festival's Bookend Award, a lifetime achievement award, at a special cer-emony during the 2000 Festival. The year before, the festival awarded the Bookend Award to Horton Foote. In 2001, two lit-

erary figures were honored with a Bookend Award for distinguished contributions to Texas literature: Pulitzer Prize–winning historian William H. Goetzmann, and Stanley Marcus, a
publisher, author, and book collector.

In 1998, the festival included an appearance by Laura's
father-in-law, former President George H. W. Bush. He spoke
about his book, *A World Transformed*, which he wrote with his
former national security adviser, Brent Scowcroft. This memoir
focuses on the major events that occurred in the first years of his
presidency, from 1989 to 1991, such as the breakup of the
Soviet Union and fall of the Berlin Wall, the massacre at
Tiananmen Square, and the Persian Gulf War.

Laura Bush didn't have to twist the elder Bush's arm to
come to Austin and take part in the festival. "He was really
thrilled to do it," she said. "Barbara Bush's main focus when she
was First Lady as well as now still is literacy, so they love the
festival," she said.[15]

The funds raised at the festival are distributed to libraries
through a grant reward system: libraries fill out an application
and apply for grants of $2,500.00. Laura stated in her press
announcements that "the Texas Book Festival's mission is
twofold. We have a wonderful annual event that gives everyone
an opportunity to experience the great range of literary talent
that Texas offers, while making a valuable contribution to
public library collections across the state." She added that the
overall definition of the festival is "a celebration of words,
reading, and published works."

Two small libraries that received grants used them to
increase their collections in much-needed areas. In Muleshoe—
the town in which Laura gave her first political speech in

1977—librarian Dyan Shipley used her grant money to buy reference materials needed by students who attended a community college. This enabled residents to study at their home library instead of making the 45-minute drive to the campus.

The size of the individual grants may not sound substantial, but according to the Texas State Library and Archives Commission, a $2,500 festival grant quite often more than doubles the annual materials budgets of many libraries. In a report on the 1999 festival, the commission also noted that they received a donation of 170 books from the festival to deliver to libraries for circulation. Most of the books were signed by authors who spoke at the Capitol during the festival.[16]

Putting on the spectacular weekend book fair is a full-time job for the organization's eleven-person staff. The festival's content and sponsorship is handled by a fifty-seven-person advisory committee and a fifty-three-person Texas Book Committee, of which First Lady Laura Bush is the Honorary Chair.

Major sponsors of the annual festival include Barnes & Noble, Microsoft, American Airlines, Austin Coca-Cola Bottling Company, Bank of America, the Brown Foundation, the T.L.L. Temple Foundation, the Susan Vaughan Foundation, Mr. and Mrs. Lee Bass of Fort Worth, Jan Bullock and Kathryn Counts of Austin, Dell, H-E-B, the Mari Marchbanks Family Foundation, and Reece West of Leakey.

During her reign as First Lady of Texas, Laura made few public appearances, especially in comparison with the Governor, who was constantly in the public eye, as the job demands. But during the weekends of the Texas Book Festival, Laura would become the mover and shaker at the Capitol.

"The festival . . . is the one time when the Bushes reverse

roles," observed the *Dallas Morning News.* "She's in charge, and he follows her around as a sidekick."[17]

"When we hear from different states about book festivals that are ongoing or festivals that are being planned, the Texas Book Festival is the greatest success story of them all," said Dr. Tydeman.

In the wake of that wild success, Laura made it a priority to take the format of the Texas Book Festival to the national stage when she became First Lady of the United States. In July 2001, she announced that a national festival would take place in September. Cosponsored by the First Lady and the Library of Congress, the National Book Festival was organized to take place in the Library of Congress and on the east lawn of the U.S. Capitol.

The plan for the National Book Festival actually sprang from a conversation between the First Lady and James H. Billington, the nation's "First Librarian" or Librarian of Congress. Billington is a graduate of Princeton and Oxford, a former history professor and director of the Woodrow Wilson International Center for Scholars, and an author.

In the first months of her move to Washington, the First Lady met Billington and they discovered that they share a common element from childhood—parents who loved books and instilled in them a love of reading.

Both James Billington and the First Lady are aware of the life-changing impact that one book can have on a life, and this common insight led to their plan to launch a national book fair in Washington.

"I am proud to join with Dr. Billington and the Library of Congress in hosting this year's National Book Festival," said Laura at the press conference in the summer of 2001. "This event gives us an opportunity to inspire parents and caregivers to read to children as early as possible and to encourage reading as a lifelong activity. I look forward to welcoming book lovers of all ages to our nation's Capitol to celebrate the magic of reading and storytelling."[18]

Unlike the Texas Book Festival, the national fair was not founded to raise funds for libraries, but primarily to celebrate authors and raise awareness about reading and literacy.

Sharing the podium with the First Lady, Librarian of Congress James Billington said, "We must all try, in every way we can, to send the message that reading is critical to our lives and to the life of our nation."

In its press release, the Library of Congress stated that the Library "and Mrs. Bush hope that the National Book Festival will encourage American families to develop a lifelong love of reading."

The National Book Festival invited the public to explore the rooms of the Library of Congress, just as the Texas festival has traditionally opened the state Capitol to visitors for readings and author panels. Activities of the one-day festival in Washington, presented on Saturday, September 8, 2001, included readings and book signings by more than forty authors and book illustrators, musical performances, storytelling, panel discussions, and demonstrations of illustration and new technologies. Attendance was free, and visitors were also treated to special tours and exhibitions in the buildings of the Library of Congress, including the Great Hall of the Library's Thomas Jefferson Building.

In the spirit of the outdoor and indoor setup of the Texas festival, the Washington festival featured pavilions set up on the

Capitol lawn in which the author readings, storytelling, book signings, book sales, and panel presentations took place.

In the Library of Congress's Madison Building, visitors attended demonstrations on the high-tech side of research and study in the National Digital Library Learning Center. The entertainment portion of the Texas festival carried over to the national event, too: Crowds listened to live music in front of the Jefferson Building and sampled food from the vendors set up across the street on the plaza of the Madison Building.

Children's book characters such as the Cat in the Hat, Clifford the Big Red Dog, and Peter Rabbit strolled the grounds as professional basketball players, including Greg Anthony from the Chicago Bulls and Pat Garrity from the Orlando Magic, appeared in the Children and Young Adults Pavilion to promote the National Basketball Association "Read to Achieve" Program.

Event areas included pavilions for History and Current Events, Mystery and Suspense, Fiction and Imagination, and Storytelling. The Storytelling Pavilion offered a wide variety of presentations, from Cuban-American stories by Carmen Deedy to an interview with two Navajo Code Talkers—World War II veterans Keith Little and Samuel Smith.

This Pavilion also served as a stage for performances of Appalachian folk music, Native American flute music, music from the South Carolina Sea Islands, and Caribbean songs. Other musical guests performing at the festival were the Monumental Brass Quintet; the Mariachi Los Amigos band; Fynesound, a Scottish/Irish music group; the Wright Touch jazz band; the Broadcreek Dixieland Band; Jinny Marsh's Hot Kugel Klezmer Band; and the Barretones Bluegrass Band.

Panel discussions throughout the day covered topics such as

"Who's That Lady? First Ladies Quiz Bowl," "Mr. Edison Makes Movies: Films by Thomas Edison in American Memory," "Children's Books, Literacy and Libraries: A Conversation," "Mystery and Suspense: Where the Bodies Are Buried," "Poetry: Hear Our Voices," "The National Library Service for the Blind and Physically Handicapped," and a Conservation Clinic with advice on preserving books, photographs, and other memorabilia.

The reading rooms housed several events such as demonstrations of the art of writing in the languages and scripts of the world, a tour of the Main Reading Room with its 160-foot high domed ceiling and stained glass, an introduction to international authors, a workshop on copyrights, and a guide to the resources available to help teachers and students use American Memory, the Library's online collection.

Exhibitions in various galleries displayed the library's national and world treasures, articles from Thomas Jefferson's library, works by renowned book illustrators, and celebrity tributes entitled "Bob Hope and American Variety" and "Here to Stay: The Legacy of George & Ira Gershwin." Visitors to the reading rooms also met Library of Congress staff members who answered questions about how to access the library's services.

❖　❖　❖

THE FIRST LADY and the Librarian of Congress prefaced the National Book Festival with a special program for fourth-grade students from a Washington-area public school. The day before the book fair, they gathered the students into the Library of Congress for a read-aloud session and a demonstration of one of the Library's Websites, *www.americaslibrary.gov*. This

"Back-to-School" program introduced the students to the First Lady and some of her favorite books, and showed them how to have fun at home or at school with an interactive Web site that is designed for families.

The first National Book Festival presented well-known, award-winning authors, some of whom have participated in the Texas event, like historian Stephen Ambrose and J. California Cooper.

The First Lady's love of mysteries was evident in the lineup of all-star writers including Patricia Cornwell, Donald Westlake, Sue Grafton, Harlan Coben, Margaret Maron, Walter Mosley, and Barbara Mertz. The young readers area was a virtual "who's who" of children's publishing, with authors such as Gary Soto, Richard Peck, Walter Dean Myers, Patricia MacLachlan, Russell Freedman, and the husband-and-wife team of Patricia and Fredrick McKissack.

To coincide with the National Book Festival, Laura announced the creation of the Laura Bush Foundation for America's Libraries. The purpose of the foundation is to update and expand the collections of school libraries across the country. According to the press release from the White House, some public school libraries contain out-of-date materials that are long overdue for replacement:

> As school budgets have become stretched, school districts have had to apply their resources to programs and services other than libraries. It is not uncommon for libraries to receive funds for computers and related technology instead of books. As a result, some libraries lack up-to-date books and reference materials. For example, the following

quotes can be found in books available in some libraries today: "Man has not landed on the moon—it can't be done." "The Soviet Union still exists." "Proper ladies wear hats and gloves and never compete with men." One of the purposes of the Laura Bush Foundation is to help libraries find a balance between technology and contemporary books by providing needed funding for book purchases.

"Connecting children with books is a critical step toward instilling the love of reading early," said Mrs. Bush. "I look forward to working with other book lovers to ensure that every child in our great nation has access to the building blocks of learning through books."[19]

The book festival in Washington was one of Laura's first major public events. With both the Texas and National Book Festivals Laura has created a vehicle for her mission that carries mass appeal and draws the attention of the press. This may be another lesson she learned from Barbara Bush, who was frustrated at the lack of publicity she received for her important literacy work during her term as First Lady. In her memoir, Barbara mused on the coverage she received for the annual ceremony of putting the star on top of the Capitol Christmas Tree.

Every year, in one of the press's favorite holiday photo ops, she would step into a cherry picker and be lifted up to the top of the tree. "It struck me that I worked so hard all year long for literacy and got little or no press coverage," she wrote, "and then I would do something frivolous like going up in a cherry picker and my picture is seen around the world."[20]

CHAPTER 9
America's New First Lady

*"The First Lady is an unpaid public servant
elected by one person—her husband."*
—LADY BIRD JOHNSON

O NE THEME DOMINATED PRESS COVERAGE about the wives of the nominees during the presidential election of 2000: How did they compare to Hillary?

In Bill Clinton's campaign for the presidency in 1992, he proudly described Hillary as his political partner, and in his acceptance speech at the Democratic Convention in 1992 he told America that a vote for him would get them "two for the price of one." Since their first days together at Yale, where Hillary received her law degree, the couple had acted as sounding boards for each other. Hillary would go on from Yale to build a distinguished career as a lawyer in Washington and Little Rock.

In his first term, President Clinton put Hillary in charge of developing a sweeping universal health-care policy, one of the primary goals of his administration. "She awed Congress with her command of the complexities of the health-care industry," wrote Margaret Truman, "when she testified before them on the Clinton bill mandating universal care." The *New York Times* described her appearance before Congress as "the official end of an era when Presidential wives pretended to know less than they did and to be advising less than they were."[1]

But Hillary's high-profile public partnership with the president opened her to all the scrutiny and hostility that comes with high office. Her years as First Lady were tarnished by scandals over the Clintons' real estate holdings in Arkansas and her own earnings from a cattle-futures investment. Thus, she became the first First Lady to be the target of her own financial scandal.

Hillary was also the target of fierce criticism over her changing hairstyles, and when she remarked about the pettiness of such coverage she was labeled antagonistic and difficult. Hillary ultimately showed them all, however, when she made a successful run for the U.S. Senate from New York and became the only First Lady in history to be elected to national office.

First Lady Hillary Rodham Clinton had broken the mold of the American First Lady, a job that remains "undefined, frequently misunderstood, and subject to political attacks far nastier in some ways than those any President has ever faced," in the words of Margaret Truman, daughter of President Harry Truman. Every First Lady has brought a unique background to the White House; comparisons between these women are moot, as there is no defined standard of expectations or duties upon which to base them. Even so, comparisons of the candidates' wives were rampant during the 2000 campaign.

Laura Bush refused to be forced to defend herself. When repeatedly asked if she would follow in Hillary's footsteps, she simply answered, "I am going to be Laura Bush."

A number of First Ladies have come to the role under trying circumstances—Lady Bird on the tragic heels of President John F. Kennedy's assassination, for example, and Betty Ford in the wake of Nixon's resignation. Gerald Ford had not even run on the ballot with Nixon, but was appointed after Spiro Agnew's resignation. The dramatic upheaval of Watergate placed Gerald Ford in the Oval Office as the only unelected president in the nation's history. George W. and Laura Bush were also ushered into the White House under sensational and historic conditions. The disputed votes in Florida ignited election mayhem that wore on for more than a month, and waiting for the outcome became a nightmare of tension and legal maneuvering for both the Bush and Gore families.

The elder George Bush summed up his daughter-in-law's behavior during that trying time. "She doesn't get all out of sorts if something isn't just right," he said. "The best evidence of that is the way she conducted herself during those awful thirty-five days when the election was up in the air. It was a savage, horrible period. But she never got rattled, never got vindictive."[2]

Laura, who had just turned fifty-four, explained that the long wait was "not really that difficult" because she and George were prepared to move on with their lives no matter what happened. "I knew George and I would be all right either way," she said. "We knew we had worked hard in the campaign, and the wait let us put our lives and even the presidency in perspective."[3]

On December 13, the day after the Supreme Court made the decision that propelled George W. into the White House, Laura went to her scheduled Texas Book Festival meeting and attended to business as usual. When the meeting broke up at seven o'clock, her husband was still working on his victory speech and waiting for the concession call from Vice President Al Gore. True to her character, Laura had the composure to sit through a two-hour meeting on a pivotal day in history and in the life of her family.

On Monday morning, December 18, 2000, Laura was driven in a limousine to the White House for her official transition meeting with Hillary. When she tried to get out of the car, the door was frozen shut, and Hillary summoned a Secret

Service agent to put some muscle to the problem. When the door finally opened, Laura stepped out of the car and the two women shook hands and posed for pictures. Laura was already familiar with the White House, having had a father-in-law as president and attended several National Governor's Association dinners there. "I feel like I sort of know it," she told the press that day. "I have slept in the Lincoln Bedroom and the Queen's Bedroom."[4]

In fact, Laura would later learn from her mother that she shared a historical link with a former occupant of the White House. In the autumn of 2001, Laura's mother decided to search out her relatives and discovered an interesting ancestor—with a connection to the American presidency—on her paternal side.

Jenna Welch recounted: "The researchers called me, asking if I had ever heard of a particular name. They told me that they found records of this man as a twenty-two-year-old infantryman during the Revolutionary War. He served at Valley Forge with General George Washington.[5]

During Laura's visit, Hillary gave her successor a tour of the living quarters and offered a few words of advice about taking advantage of her time as First Lady. Among her suggestions was that Laura carefully consider all the invitations she would be receiving, so as not to miss an opportunity that she may later regret.

The actual move was simpler than most because, on the advice of her mother-in-law, Laura didn't bring any furniture from Texas. The Bushes did bring their three pets: Barney, a Scottish Terrier Laura received a few weeks earlier from George on her birthday; Spot, the eleven-year-old dog offspring born in the White House to famous First Dog, Millie; and the family cat, India.

The only pet that didn't make the move to the White House was the Bushes' other cat, Ernie, a six-toed cat they took in as a stray in 1998. Laura feared that he would rip up the antique White House furniture, and they orphaned him out to their good friend, Brad Freeman, in Los Angeles. Ernie's short-lived escape from Freeman's house made the front-page news in late 2000.

In the midst of her packing and arranging for the inauguration in late December, Laura was suddenly sidetracked by illnesses in her immediate family. On Christmas Day, her nineteen-year-old daughter Jenna complained of a stomach ache that worsened by late afternoon. George and Laura rushed her to St. David's Hospital in Austin, where she was diagnosed with appendicitis and immediately taken to surgery.

Only the week before, Jenna's grandmother and namesake, Jenna Welch, suddenly took ill. She had been staying at the Governor's Mansion for the holidays, and on Wednesday told the family that she felt very lightheaded. They took her to Brackenridge Hospital where, after running several tests, no physical problems could be detected. Although her mother's condition was worrisome for Laura, she was relieved to hear that by the next afternoon Jenna felt well enough to be released.

Once again turning her attention to settling in, Laura decided to make only one major change: She moved her office back to the East Wing where the First Lady's office had traditionally been housed. Hillary Rodham Clinton had moved her offices to the West Wing to be closer to the nerve center of the administration.

Then, just two weeks after the inauguration, Laura surprised Washington society by leaving town for two full weeks to work on the family's new ranch in Crawford, Texas. Rather than begin a series of lunches or parties, she had decided to go back to her home state to focus on her first priority, her family.

"I think I can help [George] also by allowing both of us to have a private life," she explained, "to get away to our ranch, to entertain friends and family members at our ranch, which gives both of us the chance to relax and visit with people."[6]

The ranch allows Laura to indulge in one of her favorite hobbies, birding, and the Bushes preserved several hundred acres of the hardwood-dotted land that they discovered, which is home to the rare golden-cheeked warbler.

Laura planted native grasses and flowers throughout the ten acres immediately surrounding the house and supervised the planting of an alley of oaks to line the long drive. At first sight, the house appears humble and small, yet chic.

"It ain't Dallas," remarked one reporter as she stepped out of her car and saw the ranch for the first time. Laura laughed and responded, "No, but we hope it's got a little Midland."[7]

"It was a true working farm—they call it a ranch—and they have some horses and longhorn cattle down there," said Laura's mother. "Someone gave them longhorns, but they're not raising cattle for sale. I think the ranch reflects true Texas because it was a working farm for many years, established by German settlers after the Civil War."

Laura's mother points out that its historical roots are attractive to the Bushes. It has also become a haven of rest and renewal for the family. "I think the ranch appeals to Laura because of its simplicity and honesty. It allows her to get back to the spirit of the soil."

Jenna Welch contends that in spite of the lure of gardening and other outdoor activities at the ranch, Laura's favorite pastime is still sitting down with a book. "Outdoorsy? Laura likes to read!" Jenna said. "But she's also a great walker. She and George, when they're down at the ranch, walk maybe three or four miles together."[8]

When it was time to move into the White House, Laura was able to turn to Barbara Bush for advice on how best to do it, as well as on how best to begin her own literacy activities as First Lady. In fact, during the campaign, one of her stock answers about how she felt about Hillary Clinton had been, "I have a favorite First Lady and it's my mother-in-law." She called this response "the perfect out," squelching the press's hunger for controversy. After election day, she also said, "I can assure you that I'll never run for Senate in New York."

Barbara Bush and Laura spent a lot of time together during George H. W.'s presidential campaign in 1992, and became very fond of each other. In the tradition of her mother-in-law, Laura does not speak on policy issues but keeps to her agenda of programs on literacy, reading, and child development.

There was one exception, however. In the first month on the job, she freely admitted that she differed from her husband on the issue of abortion. In her January 18, 2001 appearance on NBC's *The Today Show*, Laura said, "I agree with my husband that we should try to reduce the number of abortions in our country by doing all of those things, by talking about responsibility, by talking about abstinence."

When the reporter asked her directly whether she thought *Roe vs. Wade* should be overturned, as her husband advocated, she replied, "No, I don't think that it should be overturned."

However, in subsequent interviews, she made it clear that she would not repeat this type of statement. "I'll be perfectly frank . . . I was not elected and George was," she told Oprah in an interview, "and I would never want to undermine him in any way. So I want to take positions on issues that I am particularly knowledgeable about and interested in."[9]

Because the First Lady's job description is undefined, it allows Laura to find her own balance between the roles of wife, mother, national hostess, and literacy activist.

"I actually think that the role is whatever the First Lady wants it to be," she said. "First Ladies have worked on issues that they were already interested in, and that's what I'm doing. Education is what I know about, and teaching is what's important to me. I think the American people think that the First Lady ought to get to do whatever she wants to do."[10]

"I want to make a difference," Barbara Bush said during her years in the White House, "and I might just as well do it by focusing on the things I'm interested in."

She didn't worry about doing the thing that would make her more politically fashionable, but rather focused on the work that she felt needed the most attention—literacy, homelessness, and AIDS. Working on her "image" or the trendiest political issue was a waste of time, she thought, because "half of the people are going to hate you anyway."

Barbara brought her sense of humor, creativity, and love of books to her fundraising efforts for literacy programs. Her book, *C. Fred's Story* (1984), an imaginative memoir of one of the family dogs, raised $40,000 for Laubach Literacy Action and Literacy Volunteers of America, and proceeds from *Millie's*

Book, the First Dog's memoirs, were donated to the Barbara Bush Foundation for Family Literacy.

"I have learned so much from watching her," said Laura. "About what it is like to live in a public house like this one. Things that have to do with how you raise your children. And she does give me advice. When there were the debates in New Hampshire last year, she said, 'Now, you know all the candidates' wives will be there, and it's best if you are the first one to speak.' I mean, it wouldn't have occurred to me. It shows what an advantage I have to have her as my mother-in-law."[11]

Besides Barbara Bush, the former First Lady whom Laura most admires is Lady Bird Johnson. She, too, was a native Texan, as well as a savvy congressman's wife who took over his office during his military service, an extraordinarily successful businesswoman, and a naturalist.

She is perhaps remembered most for her highway beautification program that blossomed out of the First Lady's Committee for a More Beautiful Capital. Later in life, she continued her work with nature conservation by founding the National Wildflower Research Center.

Lady Bird, born Claudia Alta Taylor and given the nickname as a small child, had a great influence on her husband and was his most crucial stabilizing force. When his ferocious temper threatened to obstruct a policy or alienate a colleague, she followed up and smoothed things out. When his moods threatened to cut short his career, she bolstered his confidence. In spite of Lyndon Johnson's well-publicized affairs, Lady Bird stayed by his side and did not go public about her feelings during his lifetime.

One of Lady Bird's primary concerns was creating a safe

haven for her husband so he would have a calm, friendly space in which to work. Laura Bush clearly shared this priority when she left Washington after the inauguration to work on the ranch and get it in live-in condition as soon as possible.

❖   ❖   ❖

ANOTHER OF Laura's priorities is keeping her daughters out of the public eye. During the presidential campaign, she took three weeks off to settle Jenna and Barbara into college. Jenna, the blond twin named after Laura's mother, entered the University of Texas at Austin, where Laura went to graduate school. Barbara, the brunette named after George's mother, followed in her father's footsteps by enrolling at Yale. Throughout their years in the Governor's Mansion, the Bushes fiercely protected the girls' privacy and never allowed them to be interviewed or photographed.

On the national stage, however, their privacy has been impossible to ensure. George and Laura's worst fears were realized in an incident early in 2001, when the press played up a story about Jenna and Barbara being cited for trying to buy alcohol at a restaurant in Austin. The drinking age in Texas is twenty-one, and the nineteen-year-old Bush girls were charged with Class C misdemeanors—Jenna for trying to use a fake ID and Barbara for ordering a margarita. A manager from the restaurant had called 911 to report the twins.

A few weeks earlier, Jenna had been fined and given an eight-hour community service sentence for buying a beer in an Austin bar. After the latest incident involving both daughters of the president, headlines quickly spread throughout the world—

the *New York Post's* "Jenna and Tonic," London's *Mirror's* "Dubya Troubya," and *People* magazine's cover story, "Oops! They Did It Again."

A few journalists went so far as to dub the affair "Margaritagate," and a national debate ensued over drinking-age laws, underage drinkers on college campuses, and whether or not it was fair for Jenna and Barbara to be publicly scrutinized for such a common citation. In Austin alone, about 500 citations are issued every year for underage drinking, and that reflects just the fraction of those who get caught. In expressing its opinion of the absurdity of America's age-twenty-one drinking laws, the *Economist* called Jenna Bush "a Joan of Arc, burning on the pyre of American puritanism," adding "there is no sillier use of the police's time than trying to criminalize a substance that has lubricated student life since universities were invented."[12]

"This is just wrong," an exasperated Laura told reporters about the relentless coverage of her daughters. "Where will it end?" The laser-beam focus on the twins continued when young Barbara traveled with her parents to Europe in July 2001. The first paragraph of a London *Times* article about the First Family's visit with Queen Elizabeth attempted to stir controversy by reporting that Barbara, in a "casual denim jacket and trousers, was not exactly dressed for lunch with the Queen. She had all the appearance of a girl travelling light, and on a last-minute whim."[13]

Infuriated, Laura felt compelled to refute with a statement to the press that her daughter actually "wore a dress." Laura told the press that she thought the coverage was "overdone" and that she regretted, as a mother, that her daughters had to endure it. "But they're doing great," she said in mid-June

2001. "They're really terrific girls."

While the media covered Jenna and Barbara's drinking story and a new spoof of the First Family, "That's My Bush," debuted on the Comedy Central channel, Laura was working behind-the-scenes to organize a summit on early childhood learning to be held in Washington in July 2001. The two-day summit, co-hosted by the First Lady; U.S. Secretary of Education, Rod Paige; and U.S. Secretary of Health and Human Services, Tommy G. Thompson, presented research and recommendations by the country's leading early childhood experts. Approximately 400 educators and representatives of government and community agencies gathered for the summit at Georgetown University on July 26 and 27.

"We all have a duty to call attention to the science and seriousness of early childhood cognitive development," said Laura in her press release about the event. "The years from the crib to the classroom represent a period of intense language and cognitive growth. Armed with the right information, we can make sure every child learns to read and reads to learn."

The title of the conference, "Ready to Read, Ready to Learn," reflected Laura's goal to provide American children with the pre-school experiences that would support their learning in grade-school. She explains her mission in a statement issued by the U.S. Department of Education:

> Some children enter school without even knowing the basics, such as the alphabet and counting. For these children, reading and learning can often be a struggle. And, it is a struggle that affects every American because if our children are not able to read, they are not able to lead.

Our challenge is to reach these children early and lift them to success. My experiences as a mother and an elementary school teacher have taught me that children that are ready to read are ready to learn.

As First Lady, I will work tirelessly to make sure that every child gains the basic skills to be successful in school and in life.

Across America, there are countless classroom heroes who are helping children beat the odds. I want to build on their success by helping to recruit more teachers, shine the spotlight on successful early childhood pre-reading and vocabulary programs, and help parents get access to information that will help them help their children learn.

Each of us has a duty to help our children achieve their full potential. By working together, we can shape the destiny of America's children with our hands and hearts.[14]

Speakers at the summit included Grover "Russ" Whitehurst, assistant secretary of education for educational research and improvement. He discussed how poverty affects a child's acquisition of pre-reading skills and outlined methods that parents and other adults can use to nurture those skills. Patricia Kuhl, co-director of the Center for Mind, Brain, and Learning at the University of Washington, explained how babies incorporate sounds in the first twelve months of life and how those early experiences inform their readiness to learn a language. "The studies show that by one year of age," she said, "infants all over the world are sorting out which sounds their language uses, what sounds can be combined in their language, and the patterns of words used in that language."

Susan Landry, Professor of Pediatrics at the University of Texas Houston Health Science Center, discussed the positive results of Head Start programs and the importance of trained intervention in this special needs population.

With this summit, Laura and the Department of Education took a major step in getting the latest early child development research to the audience that can most benefit from it, early-grade teachers and parents. "Good teachers need the support of people like you, the experts," she told the audience in Washington. "They need to know what you know about early childhood and language development."

The First Lady's reading and early childhood initiative is built on three basic platforms: "Bringing What Works to Parents," "Tools to Teach What Works," and "Recruiting the Best and the Brightest." The first area involves getting parents to read to their children at the earliest age possible. In most of her public appearances, Laura appeals to parents to read to children early and often to give them the best chance to succeed in all school subjects.

"In 1998," she stated, "in our highest poverty schools, 68 percent of fourth graders could not read at the basic level. Over the last fifteen years, 15 million students have graduated from high school without the ability to read at the basic level."

One of the programs that gets parents involved in early childhood reading is Reach Out and Read (ROR), a hospital/clinic–based program launched in Boston that provides free books and reading tips to parents during visits to the doctor. Laura launched sixty ROR programs in Texas during her tenure as First Lady, and is now highlighting the program as part of her national initiative.

The "Tools" component of Laura's initiative involves bringing cognitive activities into Head Start and other pre-school programs. "Through scientific research," she said, "we have learned a great deal about the way children learn to read. Education experts agree that we should incorporate stronger pre-reading and vocabulary activities in pre-kindergarten programs." Laura also supported this type of program in Texas and included it in the child development legislation she helped create in her home state.

"Recruiting Teachers" is critical in today's era of teacher shortages, and Laura promotes three programs that tackle this issue. "Right now, in this economy, teachers don't make as much as [those] in other jobs, which is why a lot of people are either leaving or not choosing the profession," she said. One of the main reason teachers' salaries are low is because we pay them with public money.

"Do they make enough money? No, of course not," she said. "Bond elections come before school districts and a lot of times they're defeated. We need to make sure everybody realizes how important it is to recruit and keep really great teachers in our schools."[15]

Teach for America is an organization that enlists recent college graduates of all academic majors to commit to two years of teaching in public schools. The New Teacher Project recruits professionals from all fields for teaching in inner-city and urban schools. Candidates must have at least a bachelor's degree and undergo an intensive teacher-training program before entering the classroom.

A third program Laura actively supports is Troops to Teachers, an incentive for retired military personnel to put their math, engineering, and science backgrounds to use in the class-room. Laura's appearances and speeches on behalf of this pro-gram have resulted in thousands of new applications from people who retired from military service and are considering taking on teaching as a secondary career.

Laura's Ready to Read, Ready to Learn Initiative focuses on the most fundamental issues facing American education. Providing very young children with an environment that nur-tures their cognitive development is important for reading readiness, and many students in inner-city schools struggle with reading because their parents did not read to them or oth-erwise stimulate their intellectual, creative, and emotional development.

Michael Kon is a teacher at Los Angeles Elementary. Ninety percent of the students at his school are Hispanic, which poses special challenges for parent participation in early child-hood reading. According to Michael,

> Part of the homework for my fifth-graders is to read aloud for a minimum of twenty minutes. . . . The biggest obstacle when it comes to parents reading to their kids," he said, "is that parents come to me and say, 'I just can't read in English.' I tell them to read to their children in Spanish, because at least they are providing aural communication. Fundamentally, they're not sound in aural communication. The kids go back and forth between Spanish and English, so they're speaking two languages and neither one fluently or correctly. If they can become fluent in one language, it makes it so much easier to carry their language and reading skills into a second language. Many of my stu-

dents are not coming in with the tools they need to succeed in school. This year only two of my fifth-grade students are in fifth-grade reading; the rest of them are in the third- and fourth-grade groups.[16]

Another inner-city teacher, Julie Polito, has worked in some of New York City's most impoverished school districts as a teacher and assistant principal, and is currently an administrator with the New York City Board of Education. Her areas of specialty are early intervention, therapeutic environments for special needs children, special education, and literacy. Among the major problems she has seen are the lack of adequate facilities for city-school children—and too few teachers. Without enough teachers, class size becomes too big to be effective. According to Julie,

City schools are physically challenged to create small, well-equipped, developmentally sound learning environments. We do not have the space, the physical buildings, or the staff to develop small schools and small classrooms that can address the needs of young children. There are many efforts to recruit teachers and it is important to train teachers well, but I don't know that we can ever train them well enough to enter into large and sometimes dangerous school environments, enlist them with overcrowded classrooms of struggling learners, pay them so little, and afford them such little respect. Without a good, basic learning environment, a teacher is forced to spend more time on the logistics of keeping a class organized and attentive than on actual teaching.[17]

Schools in America's major urban centers have greater challenges than most, and the First Lady's child development initiative is targeted at those areas as well as schools in small cities and rural areas. In her speeches about her childhood initiatives, Laura also talks about her war against what she calls "aliteracy." This term applies to "people who can read but don't read, but instead only watch TV or play computer games," she said. "I hope we can also combat aliteracy as well as illiteracy.

"We already know a great deal about how we can provide children from all racial, ethnic, and socioeconomic backgrounds with the skills and knowledge they need to prepare them for success in our elementary and secondary schools," Laura stated prior to her Washington summit. "We also know that too many homes and too many classrooms around the country do not have the information to take advantage of the latest research. We hope that this summit will help us to begin the process of building bridges of opportunity between the research and the children who will most benefit from it."

❖   ❖   ❖

DURING HIS gubernatorial campaigns, George W. often remarked that his wife had become more popular in Texas than he was. A poll taken sixth months after the Bushes moved into the White House showed that this was true on the national level as well. In fact, sixty-four percent of those polled said they had a favorable opinion of Laura, whereas 61 percent said they had a favorable opinion of the president. The poll, created by the Pew Research Center for the People and the Press, questioned 1,003 adults in July, 2001, and also revealed that Laura had a slightly higher approval rating than Hillary Rodham Clinton when a similar poll was conducted at the end of Hillary's first six months as First Lady (64 versus 60 percent).[18]

Support for the First Lady was unevenly spread in the poll: her approval among those under the age of 30 was 53 percent and among those over the age of 50, 73 percent. Divided into party lines, 87 percent of Republicans gave her a favorable rating, while only 54 percent of Democrats did so. When asked which First Lady has best embodied the role, Nancy Reagan, Barbara Bush, and Hillary Rodham Clinton won more votes than Laura in the poll.

Of course, it was an early rating, and, according to the editor of the Pew poll, Laura had not yet had time to make "a strong impression on the American people." Overall, however, the survey confirmed what George had predicted would occur: "As America gets to know her, they will love her as I do."

On August 29, 2001, eight months into her term as First Lady, Laura's growing national popularity was made evident with her acceptance of the American Legion Auxiliary Woman of the Year Award. At the ceremony held in San Antonio, she made a brief speech that highlighted the Auxiliary's work with a children's reading program:

> These women are leaders whom I respect and admire very much . . . people such as Governor Christine Todd Whitman, Elizabeth Dole, and, of course, the incomparable Erma Bombeck . . . who was a great lady. She said, "When I stand before God at the end of my life, I would hope that I would not have a single bit of talent left and could say to Him, 'I used everything you gave me.'"

Laura went on to praise the women in the room, whose talents and abilities had made a difference in the lives of so many. She closed with a final reference to Erma Bombeck, whose wholesome wit and wisdom was obviously close to Laura's heart. She quoted Bombeck: "Children make your life important." Laura went on to say, "They really do, and President Bush and I will never forget that—that's what motivates us and shapes our goals and efforts for the future. So on behalf of the children of America, I accept this award."

❖   ❖   ❖

LAURA WELCH BUSH came to the White House as her own person. She does not like to shop, is not interested in clothes, wears everyday Cover Girl makeup from the drugstore, and therefore will not be a fashion-plate First Lady in the tradition of Jacqueline Kennedy—even though one reporter was compelled to write that "her loveliness is almost startling." She talks about issues with her husband but will not air her opinions in public or push a high-profile political agenda through her husband's administration as did Eleanor Roosevelt. She is resolved to make a difference in the areas she knows well and to make the best use of her national forum, unlike First Lady Mamie Eisenhower, who once mused, "Ike runs the country, and I turn the lamb chops."

Thanks to the experience of previous campaigns and lessons learned from her in-laws, Laura has developed a steady center that helps her handle the criticisms directed at her husband. "She seems to handle it very well," said her mother, "and she doesn't take it personally. It won't get any easier. But she knows that that goes with the job. She's gained so much by seeing Barbara and George in the same position, and she's learned from her mother-in-law how to do her job."

Jenna also believes that Laura will maintain her priorities and not be swayed by social or political pressures to become someone she is not. "I think she'll just always be like she is," said Jenna. "Some of the presidents' wives have been younger, but most have been women in their middle years like Laura whose personality is formed and not subject to change."[19]

Laura Bush is content being Laura Bush, using her time in Washington to celebrate literature and help parents and educators benefit from the latest research in child development and learning. From her days as an A-student at Lee High School to her tenure at the Capitol in Austin, she has always made the best possible use of her time and her resources. America should expect nothing less of her years in Washington.

"I have a forum," she said in her first week at the White House. "I won't have it always. The time is now."[20]

CHAPTER 10
The Lady in Red

"I don't know that I'm trying to say anything with my appearance. I hope I'm saying something with my actions."

—FIRST LADY LAURA BUSH

"SIMPLE ELEGANCE" is probably the phrase that best describes Laura Bush. About 100 days after moving in to the White House, the First Lady appeared in *People* magazine's "50 Most Beautiful People in the World" issue. The article highlighted her preference for simple tastes in dress and makeup.

"I have a lot of contrast with dark hair, blue eyes, and fair skin," she told the reporter, "and I think people with a lot of contrast look better with less, so that's what I like.'"[1]

But when Laura is on the ranch in Texas, she dresses like every other ranch wife. "I wear jeans and a shirt," she said. "I fix my hair and put on makeup, and I don't touch it all day." Even in Washington, where she shuttles between the White House and various functions to promote her education programs, she carries a plain handbag filled with just the basics. "Just like every other woman in America, I carry a lipstick, a hairbrush, and Altoids," she has been quoted.

Her grooming at the White House is more detailed than her routine back at the ranch, however. Before special events and public appearances, a team of hair stylists goes into action and preens her between clicks of the cameras. Laura laughs about all the attention and admits that it's pleasant to be fussed over for a change. "I'm enjoying that, I really am," she said. "It's a luxury. It's not hard to get used to."

Laura has worn her hair short most of her life, and at times her daughters speak up about a hairdo they consider too stiff. "My daughters used to advise me to do something about it because it moved as a unit," she said. "Teenage girls love to make a mother humble."

From her Inaugural Ball gown to her daily suits, Laura is outfitted by her longtime Texas designer Michael Faircloth. When the voting ordeal of November and December 2000 was finally over and Laura knew she would be attending the Inaugural Ball, she called Faircloth and put him on notice: "We have to get started," she told him. Laura had depended upon the designer's slim suits with sharp shoulders throughout her years as First Lady of Texas, and she had every intention of staying with him for her move to the White House.

Forty-one-year-old Faircloth, whose name appears to have predestined him for his job, was thrilled with her decision. Designing for the First Lady would put him more firmly on the map of his profession. "I've always wanted to have a place as an American designer," he said. His 300 active clients include society ladies, debutantes—and the Dallas Cowboys cheerleaders, for whom he has designed uniforms.

Laura's mother-in-law, Barbara Bush, had chosen another designer, Arnold Scaasi, to dress her tastefully during her years as First Lady. Scaasi offered a very different look for Laura's mother-in-law, and developed Barbara's trademark "Barbara blue" for many of her outfits. "We created a look that fit the image of the White House and her job in the White House," said Scaasi, "and that she felt comfortable in."

Although Laura appears more robust on television, Faircloth describes her as "a curvaceous size eight," and adds that she has been the same size for all the years he has known her.

"She maintains her weight beautifully. There's no fat closet or skinny closet," he said.[2]

The designer recalled that when he first met Laura in 1994, she was "very kind, a little bit reserved. All of this was very new. She didn't wear formal clothes on a daily basis. She was very casual."

The personal style that was developed for Laura evolved out of the exacting demands of television and campaigning, not out of personal preferences in color or cut. Laura had grown to love wearing subdued tones like camel and gray, but was compelled to switch to bright colors like blue, purple, and yellow that "pop" on television.

Jackets had to be styled short so that she wouldn't sit on and wrinkle them before standing up to give a speech. Blazers had to be button-down so she could wear them without a blouse, which cut down excess bulk and offered a sleeker look.

Faircloth, a self-described minimalist who, like Laura, is fond of charcoal gray, molded his client's look to meet the unique requirements of her wardrobe. Her clothes, especially the high-profile outfits for the inaugural week, had to stand out so the new First Lady could be "seen from the back row."

For the swearing-in ceremony, for example, he created a peacock blue cowl-neck tunic and slim skirt with a matching wool coat. He felt that something in dusky olive or sage would have perhaps been more sophisticated, but television required bright colors. Laura's inaugural wardrobe also included a cranberry dress; two suits, one pink and one green; and two evening gowns, one champagne and one teal.

On January 4, 2001, the First Lady's inaugural gown became national news when *Women's Wear Daily* ran a cover story entitled "First Lady in Red." Writer Rusty Williamson described Faircloth's studio as the "hottest little atelier in Texas," and stated that the designer had a hunch that the soon-to-be First Lady would go for red for her gown.

"It took less than thirty seconds for Laura to say yes when she saw the sketch of the red evening dress after looking at maybe a dozen other possibilities," said Faircloth. When finished, the Chantilly lace dress featured thousands of Austrian crystal beads that took three seamstresses 100 hours to sew onto the fabric.

"It's glamorous but it's not beaded with reckless abandon," Fairchild said. He also created a red silk satin evening coat with sky-blue lining and floral beading that matched that of the gown. To accompany this ensemble, a beaded, red satin evening bag was hand-made by the Judith Leiber company.

Carrying a Judith Leiber bag to the inaugural ball has become a tradition with First Ladies since Pat Nixon chose one in 1969. Laura chose a ruby and diamond necklace to adorn her scarlet gown.

The outfit was a success, and style aficionados were impressed with the First Lady's choice for her inaugural ball gown.

The job of outfitting nineteen-year-old twins Barbara and Jenna Bush for the inauguration was given to a Bush family friend, ready-to-wear designer Lela Rose of New York. Lela's husband, Rusty Rose, was one of George W.'s partners in the Texas Rangers baseball team, and the couple have been friends of the Bushes for many years.

"It's a lot of honor and a lot of luck to be designing for the Bush daughters," Lela said. "They're twins, but they're nothing alike in terms of appearance. Barbara is very interested in fashion and has very classic tastes. Jenna is a little more fun-loving and a little more into the trends." The twins had worn Rose fashions before, but this would be the first time they had her design outfits just for them.

For Barbara, Lela created a flared pink leather jacket to wear over a black-and-white wool houndstooth sheath dress with a matching overcoat. Jenna sported a long camel and ivory checked skirt with a moss green cashmere sweater. In anticipation of a chilly Washington evening, her ensemble included a long camel coat that matched the skirt. "For the inauguration," said Lela, "we needed to find something in-between, styles that aren't too suity but fun and young."[3]

Michael Faircloth hand-delivered Laura's gown and inaugural wardrobe to the family ranch in Texas before the Bushes left for Washington. He wanted his precious cargo to be closely guarded by the Secret Service.

"I know Laura and her taste really well," Faircloth said. "It's all about classics and interpreting them for her style. She's an extremely intelligent woman with lots of self-confidence, and she knows what works for her. And I think that personal style will continue to evolve after she goes to the White House."[4]

According to Laura's mother, not all of the First Lady's outfits come from a designer's shop. A good section of the wardrobe hanging in her White House and Crawford closets come right off the rack.

Just how important is a First Lady's sense of style? "Of course, the First Lady should be fashion-conscious," said Boston designer Alfred Fiandaca, who created some pieces for Lady Bird Johnson's wardrobe in the 1960s. "We want to take pride in the appearance of our leaders."

World-famous designer Oleg Cassini mused, "I think the American people are frustrated that they don't have a king and queen. It starts from there." Cassini designed much of Jackie Kennedy's trend-setting wardrobe during her tenure in the White House. "Every First Lady enters the White House with an imperial stature," he added. "It depends on her ability to sell that point. She's either first class or she's not. Mrs. Bush can do a tremendous amount for the fashion world, if she decides she wants to go in that direction."

There is no question that dressing the part of the First Lady is often challenging. "No matter what she does," said Edith Mayo, curator emeritus of the Smithsonian's First Ladies exhibit, "she'll offend some segment of the public. If she tries to please everyone, she'll just be criticized for having no mind of her own."

❖ ❖ ❖

INTERESTINGLY, the First Lady's style has been a news-worthy topic since Mrs. Washington gave her first official din-ners in old New York. During those very formal evenings, George and Martha entertained in a way befitting a new republic that sought to be recognized as an equal with its Euro-pean peers. Martha's gracious personality was legendary, and was instrumental in achieving the respect of the international community.

In the 1920s, America had an elegant, extremely attractive First Lady who perfectly fit the bill for the slender fashions of the day. Grace Coolidge certainly did justice to beautiful clothes, and her husband, President Calvin Coolidge, "urged her to spend so much money on clothes, his reputation for frugality would have been permanently exploded if the reporters had told all they knew," wrote Margaret Truman.

"His favorite hobby was buying clothes for Grace," she continued, "[and] he often went shopping with her and was not hesitant about expressing his opinion about what looked good on her and what didn't."

Another president who fussed over his wife's wardrobe was Lyndon Johnson, who continually commented on Lady Bird's looks and demanded she always wear makeup and fresh lipstick.

Nancy Reagan was severely criticized for her stylish wardrobe as well as her redecorating of the White House. Daughter of a New York actress and film star in her own right, Nancy strove to bring the best of everything to the White House and make it a "special place" in American culture. Pundits gleefully wrote about her glamorous Hollywood excessiveness, even though all of Nancy's gowns were donated by top designers and, in Nancy's view, gave her the opportunity to do something good for the fashion industry.

All of the money spent on redecorating—and purchasing new china—was donated by Republican supporters, and not a penny of taxpayers' funds had been used. This fact did not come out in the press, however, as Nancy had become a favorite target by those in the press who had dubbed her Queen Nancy.

Conversely, two decades earlier the press had expressed unbridled adulation toward a First Lady with a high sense of style. In the 1960s, Jacqueline Kennedy enthralled reporters, television producers, the American public, and the world with her wardrobe and devotion to transforming the White House into a palace of democracy.

In an inspired move, she asked Paris-born designer Oleg Cassini to create a Washington wardrobe that would befit the French aristocracy, asking him to design dresses that "I would wear if Jack were President of France." The result was no less than a global fashion trend—the "Jackie look."

Unlike Jackie, Hillary Rodham Clinton arrived at the White House with her priorities focused on the political arena, rather than in the cultural and fashion worlds. She paid for it in the press with a riotous focus on her ever-changing hair styles and clothing choices. For most of her life Hillary had enjoyed wearing her hair differently from week to week, but in the national spotlight she was forced to explain herself. "Anyone who's looked at pictures of me," she said, "going back to when I was in high school, knows I change my hair all the time. I did that long before I was in the public eye. I try different types of clothes. I don't take it seriously. . . . I think it's fun."[5]

Many American women were mystified by the press's obsession with Hillary's headbands and whether or not her hair was flipped in or out. As Barbara Bush discovered in her many years of public life, a First Lady will never please everyone, and perhaps no other First Lady has come under attack on so many levels—her hairdos no exception—as Hillary Rodham Clinton.

Laura Bush shares Hillary's sentiment in that respect. She has no desire to remake her image as a result of her role as First Lady. She is content with her hair, her simple makeup, and the clothes designed for her by Faircloth. Any other choices, in her view, would be artificial. And, as anyone who knows her will confirm, Laura Bush is anything but artificial.

First Mother:
September 11, 2001

"When terror struck, Laura Bush . . . almost instantly became the First Mom, comforting and reassuring the entire nation."
—NEW YORK POST,
SEPTEMBER 23, 2001

As the disastrous events of September 11 brought terror and sadness to everyone in the nation, the President and First Lady, like everyone else around the world, mourned the lost and injured, and wondered, *What will happen to this nation? Are we still in danger? How can I help?*

The next day, a Laura Bush few Americans really knew emerged as a visible symbol of America's need to reach out to victims of the disasters. She acted swiftly, joining Dr. Bernadine Healy, President and CEO of the American Red Cross, and the two women visited D.C.'s local blood donation centers. Immediately afterward, she dropped in on the Walter Reed Medical Center to speak to those hospitalized from the Pentagon attack. She had two objectives, both of which she accomplished, as she told reporters outside the hospital.

> Besides having a chance to visit with three of the victims who are here at Walter Reed, whose lives will be changed forever like all of ours . . . I also had the chance to thank the emergency team members. . . . I know how tough it is for them just like it is for the patients who are in here. . . . All of us as Americans have the opportunity to show our compassion, our resilience, and our courage.
>
> That's what these members of the team behind me showed America yesterday as they rushed to the Pentagon to rescue people. It also gives us all a chance as Americans

to do what we can for our fellow Americans, to donate blood in cities where they need an adequate supply.[1]

The First Lady continued on, offering a message that Americans would soon associate with her—the need to reassure America's children. "It's a time for parents to make sure their young children don't spend a lot of time in front of the television," she told those outside the hospital.

"This is a good time for us to think about the message that our children are getting everywhere. Let them know that most people in the world are good and this is a rare and tragic happening, but let them know they are safe and are loved all over the country."

Her compassion was coupled with gratitude to the press for their responsible handling of the tragedies. "I also want to thank the media for the way you are covering all of this," she said, "for the respect and dignity you are giving victims and the people all over our country who are suffering."

Later that day, Laura sat down and wrote two letters that would soon arrive at the offices of every state school superintendent in the country. Addressed to America's students, each one was carefully written to convey her message of trust and support in words that were appropriate for two age groups.

A Letter to Elementary School Students
from Laura Bush

Sept. 12, 2001

Dear Children:

Many Americans were injured or lost their lives in the recent national tragedy. All of their friends and loved ones are feeling very sad, and you may be feeling sad, frightened, or confused, too.

I want to reassure you that many people—including your family, your teachers, and your school counselor—love and care about you and are looking out for your safety. You can talk with them and ask them questions. You can also write down your thoughts or draw a picture that shows how you are feeling and share that with the adults in your life.

When sad or frightening things happen, all of us have an opportunity to become better people by thinking about others. We can show them we care about them by saying so and by doing nice things for them. Helping others will make you feel better, too.

I want you to know how much I care about all of you. Be kind to each other, take care of each other, and show your love for each other.

With best wishes,
Laura Bush

A Letter to Middle and High School Students
from Laura Bush

Dear Students:

On Sept. 11, 2001, many Americans lost mothers, fathers, sisters, brothers and friends in a national tragedy. Those who knew them are feeling a great loss, and you may be feeling sorrow, fear and confusion as well.

The feelings and thoughts that surround this tragedy are as plentiful as they are conflicting. I want to reassure you that there are many people—including your family, your teachers, and your school counselors—who are there to listen to you.

September 11 changed our world. But with each story of sorrow and pain comes one of hope and courage. As we move forward, all of us have an opportunity to become better people and to learn valuable lessons about heroism, love and compassion.

As we mourn those who died, let us remember that as Americans, we can be proud and confident that we live in a country that symbolizes freedom and opportunity to millions throughout the world. Our nation is strong, and our people resilient. We have a well-earned reputation for pulling together in the worst of times to help each other.

I send my best wishes and my hope that you will always take care of your family, friends, neighbors and those in need.

Sincerely,
Laura Bush

❖ ❖ ❖

ON THE THIRD DAY after the tragedy, with the body count in downtown New York rising and bomb threats at the Empire State Building and elsewhere taxing an already exhausted and depleted police force, Laura attended the president's address to the nation from the senate chamber. Flanked by British Prime Minister Tony Blair and New York Mayor Rudolph Giuliani, Laura exchanged reassuring glances with her husband who glanced up to her during periods of applause. Amidst the President's passionate vows that justice would be done was his obvious need for the support of the nation—and his First Lady.

On Wednesday and Thursday, Laura and the president put their heads together to organize a televised prayer service to be held at the Washington National Cathedral on Friday. Millions of Americans, still reeling in shock from Tuesday's attacks, gratefully tuned in to a deeply moving ceremony that included prayers from religious leaders of many faiths and a sermon by the Reverend Billy Graham. The president had urged the nation to make Friday a day of prayer, and those who did not go out of their homes to gather at a local church, synagogue, or mosque were able to share in this memorable service from Washington.

Among the nation's political leaders attending the service were four former presidents: Bill Clinton, George H. W. Bush, Jimmy Carter, and Gerald Ford. From the start, the "National Day of Prayer and Remembrance Interfaith Gathering" moved and comforted viewers with words such as those from the Washington Bishop, Jane Holmes Dixon, who said, "Those of us who are gathered here—Muslim, Jew, Christian, Sikh, Buddhist, Hindu—indeed, all people of faith—know that love is stronger than hate."

Prayers, scripture readings, and music filled out the service, including anthems by the Cathedral Boy and Girl Choristers and the United States Navy Sea Chanters, congregational hymns, and two songs, "America the Beautiful" and "The Lord's Prayer," sung by American opera star, mezzo-soprano Denyce Graves.

In his sermon, Reverend Dr. Billy Graham described the nation's foundation that cannot be destroyed by terrorists or anyone else:

> We all watched in horror as planes crashed into the steel and glass of the World Trade Center. Those majestic towers, built on solid foundations, were examples of the prosperity and creativity of America. When damaged, those buildings eventually plummeted to the ground, imploding in upon themselves. Yet, underneath the debris, is a foundation that was not destroyed. Therein lies the truth of that old hymn that Andrew Young quoted, "How Firm a Foundation . . ." Yes, our nation has been attacked, buildings destroyed, lives lost.
>
> But now we have a choice: whether to implode and disintegrate emotionally and spiritually as a people and a nation—or, whether we choose to become stronger through all of this struggle—to rebuild on a solid foundation. And I believe that we are in the process of starting to rebuild on that foundation. That foundation is our trust in God.[2]

The balm of beautiful music at the Cathedral prayer service brought tears to the eyes of President Bush and many others. Susan Graham, a native of Laura's hometown, participated in a memorial service in New York's Riverside Church and commented on the Washington service. The West Texas opera star noted the important role of musicians in doing their part to heal the country with their special gifts:

> The events of September 11 have left us all shocked, stunned, dazed and confused, scared and reluctant to venture forth. In all the church/synagogue services, however, the prevalence of music has proven to be a healing power of the most instinctive primitive order. The sight and sound of hundreds of people standing to sing all six verses of "A Mighty Fortress Is Our God" at Washington's National Cathedral was very moving indeed. It is to that order that many of us as musicians are called to the fore. We are not firefighters or rescue workers or doctors or investigators, but what we have can minister to the souls of the living.[3]

The day of the service at the National Cathedral, Americans throughout the country attended their own prayer services and memorials. In Laura's hometown, bells chimed at noon to call people in to a prayer service at the First Presbyterian Church where the Bush family worshipped when George was growing up. Laura's mother attended the service held at First United Methodist and was interviewed by a local Midland television station on her way back to her car.

Like everyone else, she felt shaken, but had confidence in her son-in-law to help the country heal. Two weeks later, she said of the attacks, "I imagine I feel as everyone else—unbelieving. I'm sure it will bring changes, we're going to have to give up some of our freedoms to come and go, there's going to be more security for travelling. That's what's sad, besides the terrible loss of life." Of her trust in the president, she added confidently, "He's a very steady person . . . we're in good hands."[4]

In the Midland schools on Friday, September 14, students and teachers observed a moment of silence. That evening, Midland College students gathered at the campus bell tower to show their support for the president and all elected officials. *The Midland Reporter-Telegram* continued work on a special edition containing short notes written by elementary-grade students to the president, such as, "God won't send us to war if you don't" and "We all love you. We know you will make the right choices."

The following Sunday, a prayer vigil was held downtown at the Centennial Plaza with patriotic music, and the next evening high school bands and choirs participated in "An Evening of Patriotism" on the steps of the Midland County Courthouse.

The Sunday following the attacks, Midland's Reverend Lane Boyd of Laura's hometown church spoke in his sermon about justice versus vengeance. He said:

> I talked about the need to pray that justice would be a part of this rather than vengeance. I described justice as the process of identifying the perpetrators, bringing them to trial, and giving appropriate sentencing. Then we'd be assured that this does not happen again. I then compared that with vengeance or revenge, which is usually excessive and inappropriate anger that leads to more hostility and more bloodshed. I encouraged people to pray for the firemen and the policemen and their families. We Christians rejoice with those who rejoice, and mourn with those

who mourn. I encouraged them to pray for President Bush and his advisers that they would have wisdom and know what is appropriate here.

Members of the First United Methodist Church extended personal letters to Washington as well. "We provided people a means by which they could write notes to the President and First Lady," said Reverend Boyd, "and also to Don Evans, the Secretary of Commerce, and his wife, Susie, who are both from Midland. We gathered the notes together and sent them to Washington. That's one of the ways we're trying to support them."[5]

On Monday, Day Six of the tragedy, the President asked Laura to travel to Pennsylvania to speak at the memorial service for the victims of United Flight 93. His instincts were excellent: Her comforting and sympathetic words revealed not only the depth of her feelings, but her ability to communicate them to the shaken members of the victims' families:

Acknowledging that the nation had just endured a week of loss and heartache of a kind none of us could have ever imagined, she quickly zoned in on the grief that "no one but loved ones could feel."

The burden is greatest, however, for the families— like those of you who are with us today. America is learning the names, but you know the people. And you are the ones they thought of in the last moments of life. You are the ones they called, and prayed to see again. You are the ones they loved.

A poet wrote, "Love knows not its own depths until the hour of parting." The loved ones we remember today knew—even in those horrible moments—that they were not truly alone, because your love was with them.

Laura reassured each and every survivor that "you are not alone. We cannot ease the pain, but this country stands by you. We will always remember what happened that day, and to whom it happened. I know many of you have felt very directly the compassion of America, both in the communities where you live and in this community where we meet. And on behalf of my husband and the nation, I want to thank every person who has reached out to you with words of sympathy and acts of kindness."

She then went on to emphasize the power of faith as an *active* force that brings hope and comfort to ease despair and sorrow. This, she said, is truly the work of those who survived.

One of last Tuesday's victims, in his final message to his family, said that he loved them and would see them again. That brave man was a witness for the greatest hope of all—and the hope that unites us now. You grieve today, and the hurt will not soon go away. But that hope is real, and it is forever, just as the love you share with your loved ones is forever.

Laura was joined at the Memorial Service by Pennsylvania Governor Tom Ridge, whom the president had just appointed as head of the newly created cabinet post of Office of Homeland Security. Together, they sought to bring comfort to the families of the forty-five victims who died when the Boeing 757 went down.

On September 18, one week after the attacks, Laura appeared on the *Oprah Show* to offer a message to America's parents. The show, entitled "How to Talk to Children About America Under Attack," gave the First Lady a national stage from which to help parents and teachers help their children through the tragedy. Her suggestions included phrases that she felt children needed to hear to feel secure during such a traumatic time:

> I think children want to hear reassurance from their parents and their teachers, "Your school is safe, you're going to be safe." The teachers want to reinforce what the parents say—that the children are loved, they are safe— and do all the things that go along in a school day.

She also suggested ways children could personally connect with those on America's "front lines":

> Children can write letters to their own firefighters and policemen in their neighborhood to thank them in honor of those that were lost.

The First Lady also recognized the incredible stress that teachers were undergoing, as they experienced the same emotional turmoil as the children they were responsible for.

> Teachers are in a very hard position. We all need to be sympathetic with our children's teachers. They are suffering exactly the same emotions we are, the sadness, confusion, the same feelings of insecurity, and they are taking

care of our children. They don't just have your own child in their classroom, they have twenty or more others.

In addition to *Oprah*, Laura appeared on dozens of television shows, from *60 Minutes* to *Good Morning America*, to spread her message about reassuring and protecting the children. With each appearance she radiated calm and compassion.

"She really believes the whole tragedy has moved her to a special place—an opportunity and a responsibility to help America get through this tragedy," said the First Lady's press secretary, Noelia Rodriguez.

Laura also worked behind the scenes to make the White House as peaceful and comfortable as possible so that her husband could do his job. "There's definitely an effort to have a routine," added Rodriguez, "a sense of normalcy, eating healthy meals, and getting rest."

The First Lady's media messages included two public service announcements recorded to air on television beginning Friday, September 21. The 30- and 15-second spots were produced with the Ad Council and reiterated Laura's commitment to spreading the message of helping America's children cope.

The shorter message read: "The tragedy of September 11th was meant to cause fear among all Americans—including our children. We can't let that happen. Talk with your children; listen to them. Tell them they are safe, and they are loved."

On September 24, Laura made an appearance at a special concert in the stricken capital. "A Concert for America" brought top entertainers to the John F. Kennedy Center for the Performing Arts in a free memorial service in honor of the victims of the September 11 attacks in New York and Washington.

The mood was somber and tearful as the audience of 2,500—families of victims, military personnel, and other grieving Washington residents—listened to gospel, jazz, and choral works in the first half, and reflective classical music performed by the National Symphony in the second half.

"Most of what we are about to play is sober and reflective," conductor Leonard Slatkin told the audience. "Every emotion that we can go through is condensed. This is our music of grief." That music included Samuel Barber's "Adagio for Strings" and William Bolcom's "Memory," with flute solo by Sir James Galway.

The First Lady's gentle words included the need to remember and appreciate the good things, such as beautiful music, during a time of crisis:

> My husband and I are proud of our fellow Americans, and the spirit of giving we've seen in this time of sadness and loss.
>
> Now, we begin to return to the good things—the things in life that bring us happiness and peace. And we find ourselves appreciating them more than ever as reminders of all the goodness and beauty in this world.
>
> Music has been called the speech of the angels, and it brings a special comfort to our nation. Tonight we are especially grateful to the artists who have gathered here at the Kennedy Center to share their talents. I thank each of you, and I look forward to an evening that we can remember and cherish.

On September 25, the day after "A Concert for America," Laura visited New York City to extend her thanks to Learning

Leaders, a volunteer organization that came to the aid of teachers and students during the crisis. Her remarks included an anecdote about one child's prescription for peace:

> I read about a four-year-old who couldn't comprehend how people can hate a whole country of people they don't even know. Her solution? She said, "Maybe we should just tell them our names." There are no limits to the outpouring of love. . . . You have a special role to play—you are there to help with the children, to offer hugs and to listen, to run errands for teachers or to help them mind their classes. You're good people of good heart, and I want to say to each learning leader here today, thank you for your efforts. Countless blessings have been revealed in the aftermath. You are one of them.[6]

Throughout all of her appearances, Laura Bush was the essence of calm and strength, even as she helped to program the national prayer service; offer practical messages to help parents, teachers, and children through the emotional trauma, and keep a loving watch over her family.

There were moments when her pain and shock were evident, when she was caught by cameras off guard, but she knew that the nation needed to see her strong, not shaken. And, according to those who have known her most of her life, Laura Bush is a vital, compassionate woman, ready and willing to meet that need.

"Over the years, friends of mine and hers have had tragedies, and she's helped us all immensely," said Pamela Nelson, a friend from Midland, Texas. "She never forgets what you're going through. And at the moment, that gets translated into being a very caring First Lady to everyone in our nation."[7]

The events on Capitol Hill and on Pennsylvania Avenue on September 11 brought panic to many, but the First Lady kept her resolve and helped her staff get through the worst.

"Some members of my staff, young women, were very afraid," she said. "The very first day, some of them just fell apart and wept all day. The second day, older members of my staff were upset, and the younger women comforted them. All the feelings we have are natural. The feelings of sadness, anger, anxiety, uncertainty, and confusion." Laura understands these natural reactions, but she is also able to keep them under control when her first priority is being strong for others.

Two weeks after the attacks, Laura's mother remarked that Laura's steadiness and serenity have always been part of her personality. "She naturally has a calm disposition," she said. "She's always been that way; she never falls to pieces. I know she would love to be able to have a healing effect on her country."[8]

President Bush, during his visit to Ground Zero in New York, told the press that his daughters were "freaked out," but "my wife's okay. She understands we're at war," he said.

The *New York Post* was the first newspaper to describe Laura as "truly the First Mother," a woman whose first instinct during the crisis was to call her children but who was just as ready to comfort, unite, and reassure her country.

When asked how she comforted her daughters in the days and weeks following the attacks, Laura said, "We tell them we love them. . . . We call every day. And if they're not there, we leave a message: 'This is our call to tell you number one, we love you, and number two, we love you.'"[9]

At this writing, the United States has launched Operation Enduring Freedom, preparing for a military course of action against the Taliban—Islamic militants who refuse to give over their leader, Osama bin Laden, the alleged mastermind behind the terrorist attacks. NATO has invoked its mutual defense clause, giving the U.S. the green light to make war against the terrorists and/or the countries that harbor them.

And, in an emotional speech to the United Nations General Assembly, New York's Mayor Rudy Giuliani urged the members to take a stand against terrorism. "The evidence of terrorism's brutality and inhumanity, of its contempt for life and its contempt for peace, is lying beneath the rubble of the World Trade Center less than two miles from where we meet today," he said. "Look at that destruction, that massive, senseless, cruel loss of human life, and then I ask you to look in your own hearts and recognize that there is no room for neutrality on the issue of terrorism."

❖ ❖ ❖

WHATEVER THE President chooses to do and whatever the outcome, Laura stands behind her husband, calmly assured, like her mother, that the country is in good hands. "He has a lot of strength of character," Laura told CNN. "He also has a lot of confidence in our country, that we're not going to be brought to our knees by something like this."

Reverend Luis Leon of St. John's Church–Lafayette Square in Washington described the First Lady's response to the crisis as "one of impeccable reassurance. . . . Her commitment . . . has been one of strength and resilience, warmth and concern, which is what we need at a time like this."[10]

Laura's predecessor, Hillary Rodham Clinton, had more praise and appreciation to extend to America's First Lady and First Mother. "I think every American has been comforted and reassured by Mrs. Bush," she said. "She has reached out particularly to comfort our children, which every one of us knows is so important at a time like this."[11]

Laura Bush faces a challenge unparalleled in our lifetime— one for which no First Lady could be prepared. As Americans begin to respond to her reassuring presence, she is becoming a familiar face on television, urging Americans to hold strong and to love their children. She has assumed the role of a beacon of hope and assurance for a grieving and shell-shocked nation.

Laura Welch Bush has surprised her constituents in the past. And there is little doubt that she will surprise the country and the world with her natural ease and sincere compassion. As Laura's spokesman, Noelia Rodriguez, said the day after the attacks on America, "You don't rule anything out when it comes to Laura Bush."

November 17, 2001

O N NOVEMBER 17, 2001, an unprecedented event in American history. For the first time, the President's weekly radio address was given in its entirety by his First Lady. Laura Bush used this opportunity to speak out against human rights abuses in Afghanistan, specifically the Taliban regime's rigid controls of women and children. In her landmark address, relayed from the Bush's ranch in Crawford, Texas, Laura outlined the abuses that made daily life an imprisoned horror for Afghan women and children.

She opened her address with a clear intention: ". . . to kick off a worldwide effort to focus on the brutality against women and children by the Al Qaeda terrorist network and the regime it supports in Afghanistan, the Taliban."

For the First Lady, this activist position was uncharacteristic. The media later reported that she had, indeed, come forward in a new way. No longer shy and academic, she was now taking on the role as supporter and defender of women's rights. After weeks of becoming newly educated about the plight of the Afghan women, Laura had decided to speak out so that they, and women everywhere, would know America's position on personal freedom, regardless of gender.

Her statistics were chilling. "Seventy percent of the Afghan people are malnourished. One in every four children won't live past the age of five . . . women have been denied access to doctors when they're sick."

Even worse, however, was the atmosphere of terror and repression that haunted the daily lives of women and children. "Even small displays of joy are outlawed—children aren't allowed to fly kites; their mothers face beatings for laughing out loud. Women cannot work outside the home, or even leave their homes by themselves," reported Laura.

She went on to describe a typical activity for which women were punished: "Only the terrorists and the Taliban threaten to pull out women's fingernails for wearing nail polish." Such practices, however, were not those of most Muslims, she pointed out. Indeed, "Muslims around the world have condemned the brutal degradation of women and children by the Taliban regime," she said. In fact, "Civilized people throughout the world are speaking out in horror . . . not only because our hearts break for the women and children in Afghanistan, but also because in Afghanistan, we see the world the terrorists would like to impose on the rest of us."

And for this reason, Laura Bush, America's First Lady, and more recently, First Mother, was speaking out against such brutality. "All of us have an obligation to speak out. We may come from different backgrounds and faiths—but parents the world over love our children."

The plight of women and children in Afghanistan was no longer simply coverage on America's news stations. Laura Bush's historic address enabled her to speak for men and women everywhere who were shocked and outraged by the Taliban's cruelty and deeply sympathetic to the women and children who were victims of these practices. From her home in Crawford, Texas, Laura's words reverberated around the world. And the world listened.

Endnotes

Prologue

[1]Transcript of the *Oprah* show, September 18, 2001.

Chapter 1

[1]Transcript of the *Oprah* show, September 18, 2001.
[2]*Vogue,* June 2001.
[3]MSNBC's *Headliners and Legends.*
[4]*Harper's Bazaar,* June 1, 2001.
[5]Author interview with Jenna Welch.
[6]Barbara Bush, *A Memoir* (New York: Charles Scribner's Sons, 1994).
[7]*Midland Reporter Telegram* Supplement, July 2000.
[8]Author interview with Jenna Welch.
[9]*Midland Reporter Telegram* Supplement.
[10]Ibid.
[11]Ibid.
[12]Author interview with Jenna Welch.
[13]*Midland Reporter Telegram* Supplement.
[14]*Harper's Bazaar,* June 1, 2001.
[15]Ibid.
[16]*Midland Reporter Telegram* Supplement.
[17]*U.S. News & World Report,* April 30, 2001.
[18]*People* magazine, January 29, 2001.
[19]Ibid.

[20]Author interview with David King.

[21]*Midland Reporter Telegram* Supplement, July, 2000.

[22]*People,* January 29, 2001.

[23]MSNBC's *Headliners and Legends,* May 2, 2001.

[24]*Oprah* magazine, May 2001.

[25]Author interview with Todd Houck.

[26]*Oprah* magazine, May 2001.

[27]Bill Modisett and Nancy Rankin McKinley, *Historic Midland: An Illustrated History of Midland County* (San Antonio: Lammert Publications, 1998).

[28]Walt McDonald, *Whatever the Wind Delivers: Celebrating West Texas and the Near Southwest* (Lubbock: Texas Tech University Press, 1999).

Chapter 2

[1]Posted at *www.goodhousekeeping.com.*

[2]Transcript, National Federation of Republican Women's Tribute to Laura Bush, August 3, 2000.

[3]*Midland Reporter Telegram* Supplement, July 2000.

[4]Walt McDonald, *Whatever the Wind Delivers.*

[5]Transcript, National Federation of Republican Women.

[6]*The Dallas Morning News,* October 29, 1999.

[7]*Detroit Free Press,* September 28, 1998.

[8]*Oprah* magazine, May 2001.

[9]*New York Times,* July 31, 2000.

[10]*Harper's Bazaar,* June 1, 2001.

[11]*People,* January 29, 2001.

[12]*Midland Reporter Telegram* Supplement, July 2000.

[13]Bill Minutaglio, *First Son* (New York: Times Books, 1999)

[14]*People,* January 29, 2001.

[15]MSNBC's *Headliners and Legends,* May 2, 2001.

[16]*People,* January 29, 2001.

[17]George W. Bush, *A Charge to Keep* (New York: William Morrow, 1999).

[18]*USA Today,* March 22, 2001.

Chapter 3

[1]George W. Bush, *A Charge to Keep.*

[2]The Petroleum Museum, *Permian Basin Petroleum Hall of Fame* (2001).

[3]Barbara Bush, *A Memoir* (New York: St. Martins Press, 1995).

[4]George W. Bush, *A Charge to Keep.*

[5]*Midland Reporter Telegram* Supplement, July 2000.

[6]George W. Bush, *A Charge to Keep.*

[7]Ibid.

[8]Bill Minutaglia, *First Son.*

[9]*U.S. News & World Report,* November 1, 1999.

[10]Ibid.

[11]Bill Minutaglio, *First Son.*

[12]Ibid.

[13]George W. Bush, *A Charge to Keep.*

[14]Bill Minutaglio, *First Son.*

[15]From the archives of *www.Texasobserver.com.*

[16]Archives of *www.Texasobserver.com.*

[17]Author interview with Todd Houck.

[18]George W. Bush, *A Charge to Keep.*

[19]*Midland Reporter Telegram* Supplement, July 2000.

[20]Transcript of *This Week with Sam Donaldson and Cokie Roberts,* December 19, 1999.

[21]Transcript of the *Oprah* show, September 20, 2000.

Chapter 4

[1]*People,* January 29, 2001.

[2]Ibid.

[3]Bill Minutaglio, *First Son.*

[4]*Washington Post,* March 30, 2001.

[5]George W. Bush, *A Charge to Keep.*

[6]*Vogue,* June, 2001.

[7]*Harper's Bazaar,* June 1, 2001.

[8]*People* magazine, January 29, 2001.

[9]Barbara Bush, *A Memoir.*

[10]Associated Press, March 5, 2000.

[11]MSNBC's *Headliners and Legends,* May 2, 2001.

[12]*Midland Reporter Telegram,* November 6, 1977.

[13]MSNBC's *Headliners and Legends.*

[14]*This Week with Sam Donaldson and Cokie Roberts,* December 19, 1999.

[15]MSNBC's *Headliners and Legends,* May 2, 2001.

[16]*Time* magazine, January 8, 2001.

Chapter 5

[1]MSNBC'S *Headliners and Legends,* May 2, 2001.

[2]George W. Bush, *A Charge to Keep.*

[3]Transcript of the *Oprah* show, September 20, 2000.

[4]Author interview with Jenna Welch.

[5]National Federation of Republican Women, August 3, 2000.

[6]*Midland Reporter Telegram,* July 2000.

[7]*Oprah* magazine, May 2001.

[8]*Texas Monthly,* April 2000.

[9]Author interview with Jenna Welch.

[10]Ibid.

[11]Transcript of the *Oprah* show, September 20, 2000.

[12]*Texas Monthly,* April 2001.

[13]MSNBC's *Headliners and Legends,* May 2, 2001.

[14]*This Week with Sam Donaldson and Cokie Roberts,* December 19, 1999.

[15]George W. Bush, *A Charge to Keep.*

[16]Ibid.

[17]*Vogue,* June 2001.

[18]Ibid.

[19]*Oprah* magazine, May 2001.

[20]*Vogue,* June 2001.

Chapter 6

[1]NPR's *Weekend Edition,* July 30, 2000.

[2]*New York Times,* July 31, 2000.

[3]George W. Bush, *A Charge to Keep.*

[4]*Houston Post,* January 17, 1995.

[5]*Dallas Morning News,* October 29, 1999.

[6]NPR's *Weekend Edition,* July 30, 2000.

[7]*El Paso Journal Sentinel,* November 3, 2000.

[8]George W. Bush, *A Charge to Keep.*

[9]Author interview with Jenna Welch.
[10]*Time* magazine, January 8, 2001.

Chapter 7
[1]*Seattle Times,* June 26, 2000.
[2]*U.S. News & World Report,* August 14, 2000.
[3]*Dallas Morning News,* September 24, 1995.
[4]*Texas Monthly,* April 2000.
[5]*Washington Post,* May 14, 2000.
[6]*Texas Monthly,* April 2001.

Chapter 8
[1]*Midland Reporter Telegram* Supplement, July 2000.
[2]*Harper's Bazaar,* June 1, 2001.
[3]NPR News, July 31, 2001.
[4]*Time* magazine, June 8, 2001.
[5]Ibid.
[6]Ibid.
[7]*New York Times,* July 31, 2000.
[8]*Atlanta Constitution,* June 4, 2001.
[9]*Time* magazine, June 8, 2001.
[10]Texas Book Festival Web site
      (*www.austin360.com/local/
      partners/texasbookfestival*).
[11]*Scribner's* magazine, February, 1927, as quoted on
      www.texasranger.org.
[12]*Austin Chronicle,* November 17, 2000.
[13]*Dallas Morning News,* July 30, 2000.

[14]Author interview with Dr. William Tydeman.

[15]Texas Book Festival Web site,
    (*www.austin360.com/local/partners/texasbookfestival*).

[16]Texas State Library and Archives Commission Web
    site, (*www.tsl.state.tx.us*).

[17]*Dallas Morning News,* July 30, 2000.

[18]Library of Congress Web site
    (*www.loc.gov/today/pr/2001/01-107.html*).

[19]*www.whitehouse.gov*

[20]Barbara Bush, *A Memoir.*

Chapter 9

[1]Margaret Truman, *First Ladies: An Intimate Group
    Portrait of White House Wives* (New York, Fawcett
    Columbine, 1995).

[2]*Harper's Bazaar,* June 1, 2001.

[3]*Time* magazine, January 8, 2001.

[4]Associated Press, December 18, 2000.

[5]Author interview with Jenna Welch.

[6]*U.S. News & World Report,* April 30, 2001.

[7]*Vogue,* June 2001.

[8]Author interview with Jenna Welch.

[9]*Oprah* magazine, May 2001.

[10]*Harper's Bazaar,* June 1, 2001.

[11]*Good Housekeeping* Web site,
    (*www.goodhousekeeping.com*).

[12]*The Economist,* June 9, 2001.

[13]*The Times,* July 20, 2001.

[14]U.S. Department of Education Web site, (*www.ed.gov*).

[15]Family Education Online interview with Laura Bush, (*www.familyeducation.com*).

[16]Author interview with Michael Kon.

[17]Author interview with Julie Polito.

[18]Associated Press, July 24, 2001.

[19]Author interview with Jenna Welch.

[20]*Time* magazine, January 8, 2001.

Chapter 10

[1]*People* magazine, May 14, 2001.

[2]*Washington Post*, January 8, 2001.

[3]*Women's Wear Daily,* January 4, 2001.

[4]Ibid.

[5]Margaret Truman, *First Ladies* (New York: Fawcett, 1995).

Epilogue

[1]*www.whitehouse.gov*

[2]Washington National Cathedral Web site: *www.cathedral.org.*

[3]Posted on Susan Graham's Web site, *www.susangraham.com/notes.htm.*

[4]Author interview with Jenna Welch.

[5]Author interview with Reverend Lane Boyd.

[6]*www.whitehouse.gov*

[7]*Dallas Morning News,* September 14, 2001.

[8]Author interview with Jenna Welch.

[9]*New York Post,* September 23, 2001.

[10]*Dallas Morning News,* September 14, 2001.

[11]*New York Post,* September 23, 2001.

Laura Bush's
Cowboy Cookies

Laura Bush's Cowboy Cookies

Ingredients:

3 cups flour
1 tablespoon baking powder
1 tablespoon baking soda
1 tablespoon cinnamon
1 teaspoon salt
3 sticks butter at room temperature
1½ cups white sugar

1½ cups packed light brown sugar
3 eggs
1 tablespoon vanilla
3 cups semisweet chocolate chips
3 cups old-fashioned rolled oats
2 cups sweetened flake coconut
2 cups chopped pecans (8 ounces)

Instructions:

Preheat oven to 350° F. Mix flour, baking powder, baking soda, cinnamon, and salt in a bowl.

In another bowl, beat butter on medium speed till smooth and creamy, about 1 minute. Gradually beat in sugars and continue beating for about 2 minutes. Beat in eggs, one at a time, and add the vanilla. Stir in flour mixture until just combined. Add chocolate chips, oats, coconut, and pecans.

For each cookie, drop ¼ cup of dough onto an ungreased cookie sheet, spaced 3 inches apart. Bake until the edges are lightly browned, about 17 to 20 minutes.

Nutrition information, per cookie:

Calories	346 (48% fat)
Fat	19 g (10 g saturated fat)
Fiber	3 g
Cholesterol	38 mg
Sodium	318 mg
Carbohydrate	42 g
Calcium	38 mg

More Famous Names from Laura Bush's Hometown

L AURA IS NOT THE FIRST NATIVE of her small hometown to reach the national stage. Midland, Texas, has been home to actor Tommy Lee Jones; Metropolitan Opera mezzo-soprano Susan Graham; screenwriter and former Saturday Night Live writer Doug McGrath; major-league baseball players Mike Stanton, Mike Timlin, and Randy Velarde; and NASCAR racer Bobby Hillin Jr. A baby girl named Jessica McClure put the town on the map in October 1987 when she fell down a tiny well and held the attention of the nation during her nationally televised three-day rescue.

Sources

Print Media

Abilene Reporter News, October 7, 1998

Associated Press, March 5, 2000; December 18, 2000;
    July 24, 2001

Atlanta Constitution, June 4, 2001

Austin Chronicle, November 17, 2000

Dallas Morning News, September 24, 1995; October 29,
    1999; July 30, 2000

Detroit Free Press, September 28, 1998

The Economist, June 9, 2001

El Paso Journal Sentinel, November 3, 2000

Harper's Bazaar, June 1, 2001

Houston Post, January 17, 1995

Midland Reporter-Telegram, November 6, 1977.

Midland Reporter-Telegram Supplement: "Aiming for
    Washington, D.C., But Rooted in Midland,"
    July 2000

New York Times, July 31, 2000

Oprah magazine, May 2001

People magazine, January 29, 2001

Permian Basin Petroleum Hall of Fame, magazine of the
    Petroleum Museum, 2001

Seattle Times, June 26, 2000

Texas Monthly, April 2000

The Times (London), July 20, 2001

Time magazine, January 8, 2001; June 8, 2001

U.S. News & World Report, April 30, 2001; August 14,
2000; November 1, 1999

USA Today, March 22, 2001

Vogue, June 2001

Washington Post, May 14, 2000; March 30, 2001

Radio/Television Transcripts

Booknotes, C-SPAN, September 13, 1992

Headlines and Legends, MSNBC, May 2, 2001

National Federation of Republican Women's Tribute to
Laura Bush, August 3, 2000

NPR News, National Public Radio, July 31, 2001

The Oprah Show, September 20, 2000

This Week with Sam Donaldson and Cokie Roberts,
December 19, 1999

Weekend Edition, National Public Radio,
July 30, 2000

Web Sites

Daily Texan Web site (*www.dailytexanonline.com*)

Family Education Online interview with Laura Bush
(*www.familyeducation.com*)

First Presbyterian Church of Midland sermon of
12/17/00, posted on *www.fpcmid.org*

Good Housekeeping Web site
(*www.goodhousekeeping.com*)

Library of Congress Web site (*www.loc.gov*)

Scribner's magazine, February 1927, as quoted on
www.texasranger.org
Texas Book Festival Web site
(*www.austin360.com/local/partners/texasbookfestival*)
Texas State Library and Archives Commission Web site
(*www.tsl.state.tx.us*)
Texasobserver.com (*www.texasobserver.com*)
U.S. Department of Education Web site (*www.ed.gov*)

Books

Berdyaev, Nicholas. *Dostoievsky: An Interpretation*. New
York: Sheed & Ward, 1934.
Bush, Barbara. *Barbara Bush: A Memoir*. New York:
Charles Scribner's Sons, 1994.
Bush, George W. *A Charge to Keep*. New York: William
Morrow, 1999.
Klapthor, Margaret Brown. *The First Ladies*. Wash-
ington: White House Historical Association, 1999.
McDonald, Walt. *Whatever the Wind Delivers: Cele-
brating West Texas and the Near Southwest*. Lub-
bock: Texas Tech University Press, 1999.
Midland County Historical Society. *The Pioneer History
of Midland County, Texas*. Dallas: Taylor Pub-
lishing, 1984.
Minutaglio, Bill. *First Son*. New York: Random House,
1999.
Modisett, Bill and McKinley, Nancy Rankin. *Historic
Midland: An Illustrated History of Midland County*.
San Antonio: Lammert Publications, 1998.

Russell, Jan Jarboe. *Lady Bird: A Biography of Mrs. Johnson.* New York: Scribner, 1999.

Truman, Margaret. *First Ladies: An Intimate Group Portrait of White House Wives.* New York: Fawcett Columbine, 1995.

Interviews Conducted by Author

Jenna Welch

Todd Houck

Reverend Lane Boyd

David King

Michael Kon

Julie Polito

Dr. Mary Lynne Rice-Lively

Dr. William Tydeman

Suggested Web Sites

The White House (*www.whitehouse.gov*)

The City of Midland (*www.ci.midland.tx.us*)

Permian Basin Petroleum Museum
    (*http://petroleummuseum.org*)

First United Methodist Church of Midland
    (*www.fumcmidland.org*)

Midland Chamber of Commerce
    (*www.midlandtxchamber.com*)

Texas Book Festival Web site
    (*www.austin360.com/local/partners/texasbookfestival*)

Library of Congress (*www.loc.gov*)

U.S. Department of Education (*www.ed.gov*)

Texas Handbook Online: An Encyclopedia of Texas
    History, Geography, and Culture
    (*www.tsha.utexas.edu/handbook/online*)

Index